TRAIN YOUR HORSE
FOR BACKCOUNTRY RIDING

TRAIN YOUR HORSE FOR BACKCOUNTRY RIDING

A COMPREHENSIVE GUIDE FOR GETTING BEYOND THE ROUND PEN

DAN AADLAND

Skyhorse Publishing

Skyhorse Publishing books may be purchased in bulk at special discounts for sales promotion, corporate gifts, fund-raising, or educational purposes. Special editions can also be created to specifications. For details, contact the Special Sales Department, Skyhorse Publishing, 307 West 36th Street, 11th Floor, New York, NY 10018 or info@skyhorsepublishing.com.

Skyhorse® and Skyhorse Publishing® are registered trademarks of Skyhorse Publishing, Inc.®, a Delaware corporation.

Visit our website at www.skyhorsepublishing.com.

10 9 8 7 6 5 4 3 2 1

Library of Congress Cataloging-in-Publication Data is available on file.

Cover design by Tom Lau
Cover photo credit: Dan Aadland

Print ISBN: 978-1-5107-2991-9
Ebook ISBN: 978-1-5107-2992-6

Printed in China

DEDICATION

For Emily, my wife, my editor and co-photographer,
and my companion on miles and miles of backcountry trails

Emily and Little Penny.

ACKNOWLEDGMENTS

Horsemanship involves an accumulation of knowledge gleaned from books, experiences, and mentors, many of whom have taught me by example. To attempt to thank all who have contributed to whatever expertise I can claim would be folly. Most recently, indispensable help in presenting the clinic called "Beyond the Round Pen: Training Your Horse for the Backcountry" (on which this book is based) has come from this remarkable crew: My wife Emily has been the catalyst, covering administrative duties as well as triple roles as assistant instructor, photographer, and clinic chef; Jennifer Hawkins Franco, our primary trainer, has been foremost in demonstrating the skills we teach as well as helping clients with individual difficulties; and trainer/ clinician Logan Gehlhausen of Pinedale, Wyoming, assisted by his delightful daughter Maddox, has contributed his considerable knowledge to the success of our mission, which has been, simply, to prepare horses and riders for the challenges anticipated in safe, gratifying interaction with equines in the backcountry.

CONTENTS

Dedication   v

Acknowledgments   vi

Chapter 1.   Why This Book?   1

Chapter 2.   Survival Horsemanship   4

Chapter 3.   Foundation Training for the Backcountry Horse   18

Chapter 4.   Basic Trail Training for Horse and Rider   42

Chapter 5.   The Neck Rein and the Side Pass   78

Chapter 6.   Walk On: Improving the Most Important
               Backcountry Gait   97

Chapter 7.   Weighty Matters: You and Your Gear on the
               Horse's Back   109

Chapter 8.   The Hunting Horse   119

Chapter 9.   Long Ears and Short Tails: A Mule Primer   135

Chapter 10.   Packing up for the Trail   146

Chapter 11.   For Want of a Nail: A Note on Shoeing   172

Chapter 12.   The Highway Trail: Tips for Trailer Training   184

Chapter 13.   The Backcountry Camp: Leave Only Tracks,
               Keep Only Memories   191

Chapter 14.   Some Essential Knots   200

Conclusion: Keep Learning, Keep Training, But Go!   221

Index   225

CHAPTER ONE

WHY THIS BOOK?

Many years ago I built a large rectangular corral out of treated posts and tough Montana fir planks. It was hard work, but pleasant. The sawn wood smelled fresh, and the view of the Beartooth Mountains to the south compensated for the strain on my tired muscles as I crowbarred my way through rocky ground to make postholes, then tamped the treated posts tightly into place. The mountains reminded me that there would be rewards ahead, rides on pine-lined trails and rocky ledges, perhaps with a moose or an elk in sight.

My plan was to build a large round pen at one end of the big corral. I'd start our colts in the pen, then move them to the larger enclosure, and eventually ride them over the foothills on our ranch. But as I neared completion of the project, I started to count the planks and posts I'd brought home from the sawmill in the bed of our old cattle truck. I was running short. Starting a cattle ranch and a horse operation on a teacher's salary meant working with a slim bank account, and I really didn't want to break from my work, killing most of a day by another drive to the sawmill.

So, my round pen shrunk. Instead of laying out the planned enclosure some fifty to sixty feet in diameter, I ended up with a modest affair scarcely thirty-five feet across from post to post. As I drove the last spike, Ralph, our farrier drove up, and I walked into the pasture to catch Rockytop, my big sorrel gelding.

Ralph eyeballed the new corral. "Nice work."

"Yeah," I said. "But the round pen ended up awfully small."

"That's just fine. With it small like that you won't stay in it very long before getting your colt out into the sagebrush where he'll really learn something."

In a sense, Ralph's remark told me what was already in the back of my mind. I had ranch work to do, cattle to move, and fences to fix in places wheels couldn't go. And, there were those mountains in the distance. The same animals that helped with ranch work would be called upon to take my family, my wife and small children, to lakes on the high plateau. Yes, my young horses would not stay in the round pen very long.

The purpose of this book is not to downplay the importance of round pen or arena work or to minimize the relevance of good groundwork. Many wonderful things can and should be accomplished between horse and trainer in a small enclosure before heading out into the sagebrush. True, many of the old-timers tended to skip all that. Once a horse had allowed someone on its back without bucking excessively (or could be harnessed without running away) the animal could go to work. Capable working companions were built this way, but probably with more stress than necessary to both people and animals.

Unfortunately for some, a funny thing happens on the way to the sagebrush: they never get there. They become so enamored with the nuances involved in building just the right relationship with their horse, with finding the perfect partnership, that they forget their original aim. Or, they lack the confidence to take the next step, to cut loose from the security blanket of corral poles or arena walls around them, and thus never do so.

Some, like a rider I heard about from an acquaintance who makes his living matching horses with clients, end up putting process ahead of the final result. The person I have in mind pined for the perfect trail horse. She'd been bucked off, she'd dealt with chargers who made her arms ache from holding them back, and she'd been generally knocked around and abused by the unruly animals she'd purchased. Eventually, my acquaintance did indeed find her a horse that was about as close to perfect as one could expect from equine flesh and blood. The gelding was gentle, willing, and smooth to ride. He rarely shied, and then did so in a mild, controlled fashion. He crossed bridges and obstacles without hesitation.

All went well for a year. Then, urged by her friends, the woman took her nearly perfect horse to a clinic featuring a particular approach involving various "games" to be played with one's horse. Though this is a perfectly good approach, it was new to the horse involved, and he was confused by it. He looked questioningly at his owner as if to say, "Don't you like me anymore? Why aren't we hitting the trails?"

Embarrassed, the woman decided to sell her horse. She had put process and method above final result. She had a jewel, but she let him go because he hadn't arrived at his level of competence by a set of methods that were in vogue among her friends. This woman, and other equine owners like her, are one of the reasons that I decided to write this book.

But the drive to offer my clinics and to write this book has another, even more important, source: a single word. The word, applicable to both horse and rider, is a simple one, seemingly forgotten by many of today's otherwise-fine clinicians. The word is "skill," or more properly, "skills." Taking equines to the backcountry, relying upon them to carry oneself and one's equipment, and restraining them safely while there, requires a broad skill set that is not taught at the average weekend clinic. Further, these skills must be honed through use; watching a brief demonstration is not enough.

Whether it's the simple task of tying a horse securely with a knot that can be untied quickly, even if it's been stressed, or the far more complicated task of securing a pack to a horse, I've found that many riders, even some with years of experience, are seriously lacking. Some routinely interact with horses in ways so potentially dangerous that it makes me shudder. Still others attend clinics of a particular school of horsemanship and become blind to the fact that it's a big equine world out there. Many things work, and the backcountry horseman should keep her or his eyes open, always be ready to learn a new approach, and not harshly judge approaches that a favorite clinician may not recommend.

In this book we'll tackle the skills for both horse and rider that we need to launch out onto those rocky mountain trails. Safety on horseback, ropes and knots, packing gear securely and safely, restraining our equines in the backcountry—all these involve skills and training. We'll get beyond those corral poles, "out into the sagebrush," as my farrier put it, and deal with the side of horsemanship too often skipped over by clinicians.

And, by training our horses for all these things we'll be training ourselves as well and hopefully having some fun along the way. Let's hit the trail.

CHAPTER TWO

SURVIVAL HORSEMANSHIP

Yes, the title of this chapter is rather ominous. That's intentional. There are far safer activities than climbing onto the back of a thousand-pound animal whose genetics tell him he'd rather escape and get that load, a possible predator, off his back. Although motorcycles are considered dangerous by many, serious injury by motorcycle riders, when apportioned to the hours of participation, are statistically less prevalent than serious injury among horseback riders. True, there may not be anything within the horse world quite as horrifying as a head-on collision on a highway, but the facts are still grim.

It's true that many of the most catastrophic equine accidents occur during robust activities such as jumping, eventing, and racing. But serious accidents occur in the backcountry, and for those, help is often far away. A good friend of mine was pitched from his horse when it shied sideways at the scent of a grizzly. Landing on a pile of deadfall, he suffered a punctured lung and multiple fractures. Luckily, good friends, modern technology (via a signal device called the SPOT), much prayer, and a gutsy helicopter crew brought him through, and he's riding today.

I, too, won't let grim statistics keep me away from horses, but I'll constantly emphasize the importance of staying safe, and much as I love my horses, I'll always prioritize the safety of humans over the animals. That's a given.

Let's start with the simple statement that horses are big, strong, and fast, and that they're capable of hurting or killing you. None is 100 percent safe. Yes, repeat after me. There is no such thing as bombproof or fail-safe among horses. Ask yourself whether you are 100 percent reliable under all circumstances, whether you've ever made a mistake, whether you've ever done something stupid. Now ask yourself whether you should expect any animal to be perfect.

I remember a conversation between my minister father, not a horseman, and Elmer, the rancher/horseman who would later become my father-in-law. Dad was just making conversation, trying too hard to be pleasant and agreeable. He said, "I suppose if you just treat a horse really well, keep him well fed, be gentle with him, he'll treat you well, too."

"He'll kill you," was the surprising reply. Then Elmer elaborated. He explained that of course you should treat a horse well, but there's a reason the old-timers say that "It's the gentle ones that kill you." They meant that gentle horses make one forget, make one skip necessary safety steps. Gentle horses rarely hurt anyone intentionally, but they're still horses. They're big and strong and fast. No matter how well trained or how well treated, when that bee stings or that big truck hits its exhaust brake, the animal might react in a way that's dangerous to you if you've completely relaxed your guard.

President Reagan used the term, "Trust, but verify," in interactions with other people. With horses perhaps we should say, "Trust, but be aware, be ready."

Let's start with the nature of the animal. Much has been made of how horses behave "in the wild," but we should remember they're domestic animals, specifically, domestic herd animals. Even those characterized as wild are, in fact, either domestic animals that have gone wild (feral) or the offspring of such. This gives us a leg up, because there's much scientific evidence that interaction with humans is actually in the genetic makeup of horses. In the fifteen to twenty thousand years of this interaction, rapport with humans has become part of their nature. Both natural selection and selective breeding by humans probably had much to do with this: the untrainable animals among them were eaten.

Thus, horses are inherently more trainable than true wild species such as elk or mountain lions or zebras. But their species did exist in a wild state for eons before humans got hold of them. That genetic memory exists as well, and it drives much of horse behavior. Horses are descended from prey animals, not predators. A horse's wide-set eyes see in nearly a full circle around him, excepting only two small "blind" areas, one directly behind its rear, the other smaller one, directly in front of its face.

Unfortunately, this eye placement has a downside, for most of the animal's vision is "monocular," not "binocular." Binocular vision is required to assess distance and depth, something horses can only do when looking straight forward. Predators like cats, dogs, and humans, by contrast, have more binocular vision, turning their heads toward objects to look straight at them.

So a horse can see to its side/rear, but not that well. The sudden appearance of a scary object will alert him, but he may not be able to instantly assess how close that object is and just how scary it happens to be. Thus the thing we horse people know as the "spook."

And why the spook? Again, horses descended from the prey end of the wild spectrum, and their major defense is to flee. They have the ability to go from an at-rest position to full flight in a heartbeat, and that's why "the gentle ones can kill you." All horses have this ability, and sometimes it defies human reason. Training, if we think about it, is primarily a matter of controlling the flight instinct, making the animal's training supersede that impulse toward sudden flight. Training aims to create a situation where that sudden, scary object results in just a start, a quick contraction of muscles, then a relaxation as realization comes that the object is not to be feared.

But though primarily a flight animal, horses will fight as well, and their primary weapons are located directly in back and directly in front. The quickness and power they have in their hind legs when kicking directly back is something you never want to feel. I had the misfortune of having to stop such a kick just once—a kick directed at a mare, not at me—but that didn't matter. I got my guard, my forearm, up in time to stop the kick from hitting my face, but at a cost. The smaller bone in my forearm snapped.

Passing the rump of a horse dictates one of two approaches: with a horse you don't know or trust, stay well back, because their reach with hind legs is considerable. With one you do know well, put your hand on the horse's back as you pass toward its rear, then keep it there as you pass very closely behind. The trusting horse that knows by your touch that you're there will likely accept your presence briefly in his rear blind spot, and in any case, you're close enough that a kick, should one occur, won't have reached its full power when it strikes you. The worst "kick zone" is from three to six feet behind the horse. At that range a kick reaches full power and velocity.

Pass close to the rear (or far back).

In front, horses have the ability to strike with their forelegs and to bite. These weapons, too, are formidable, and you'll see them in action when you watch herds of horses in "play." It's rough stuff. Rapport with your horse means neither the front nor rear weapons are likely to be used against you— at least *intentionally*. Aye, there's the rub.

But there's a safe zone, an area near the horse's body where the animal can see us perfectly well and where, during a sudden spook, it can't strike out. This safe place is the shoulder area and thus the area where we should center our activities. Always approach any horse you don't know extremely well at the shoulder, not from the front or back. From any position, you should speak softly and make yourself known. But as a rule go toward the shoulder, not the face.

I'm amazed at the number of people visiting our ranch who rush directly to a horse's face, just as they would toward their dog. Dogs and cats, predators by nature, can see you coming. The horse's tendency, particularly with a stranger, is to pull back so that he can see you better. Remember that blind spot? That's just the place our visitors often invade when they move quickly toward the animal's face.

And that pullback tendency gives rise to another sort of accident, one that becomes especially likely when you duck under the lead rope of a tied horse in order to get to his other side. If he's used to it and knows you're there, okay—but startle him in this position and two things happen, both bad. First, the horse pulls back, reaches the limit of his lead rope, and then jumps forward with front feet elevated. And on a bad day, you're squarely under those front feet. This accident is too common, particularly in the confines of a trailer.

Approach at the shoulder and gently place your hand on the animal's withers, the high, bony place at the rear of its neck. This is a place the horse can't reach to scratch, and they like a hand in this place. It seems to soothe

Approach at the shoulder with a hand on the withers.

them, and as they relax they appreciate a gentle massage of this area. Depending on the animal, where he is in training, and his trust of you, simply standing there with your hand on this spot, will usually bring on a state of relaxation.

That hand on the withers has another benefit. Watch basketball players "in the paint" (under the basket) and you'll notice a defending player sometimes touches the shoulder or back of the player he's guarding. This is legal as long as he doesn't impede that player's motion. I asked my son why he did this during a high school game, and he thought a moment, then said, "Well, I can tell by the touch what he's likely to do next, feel it just as it starts."

Similarly, that hand on the withers is in contact with the horse's muscles and nerves. If he's excited or worried, you'll feel that, though perhaps on a subconscious level. If he's about to move, you'll tend to feel that as well.

In discussing rapport with a horse, the word "trust" is frequently used. But I'm not sure we take enough time to examine what that really means. I write this shortly after the devastation to the Houston area by Hurricane Harvey. There have been the usual interviews of folks in shelters set up for those flooded out. The adults looked harried and resigned, but the children, in telling their experiences to reporters, were often animated and excited, even happy. Why? Trust on its most basic level is primarily a manner of personal safety. Children of the hurricane trusted their personal safety to the hands of their parents and the police, firemen, and volunteers doing the rescuing. That relieved them of a tremendous burden their parents had to bear.

Sophisticated nuances of trust can come later, but the basic one with horses is simple. When working with a horse, we're asking the animal to give up its regular and most-common defense—running away—to a human handler who will tie him to something solid and eventually go up onto his back, just where a predator would land. Instincts tell him those things endanger his personal safety, but you, as his handler, are asking him to believe that you'll take over those safety concerns. Throughout our interaction with the animal we must remember just what we're asking. Are we presenting ourselves in a manner we would trust if seen through the animal's eyes?

Often "partnership" with a horse is stressed, and there is something to that as long as you, the human, remain the senior partner. But for the most part, a horse put into a new situation isn't looking for a partner. He's looking for a parent.

When we progress to handling this horse, to haltering and leading, again it's best to work at the shoulder or base of the neck. There's no need to place a halter (or later, bridle) in front of the animal's face. Instead, between two fingers grasp the portion of the halter that leads over the poll to the buckle (or loop, if it's a tie halter). Hold the rest of the halter loosely in your hand. Slide your hand and the halter from the withers to the base of the neck and simply drop the halter, all but the strap you've retained, over on the far side of the neck. Slide up toward the ears, pick up the halter with your left hand in front of the horse's nose, and slide it up in place. Finally, buckle or tie.

When haltering drop the halter over the horse's neck holding on to only the top strap.

Slide it up over his nose.

Buckle it in place.

Haltering this way, from the shoulder and near side of the neck, never puts you into the danger zone in front, and it keeps the horse relaxed. And, when it comes to leading this haltered horse, the safe place continues to be just at the juncture between his neck and shoulder. This has been the traditional posture for leading an animal since Xenophon prescribed it nearly 2,500 years ago. If a horse so led wants to charge ahead of me he gets a sharp elbow in the chest. I want him to walk at the pace I set, like a dog well-trained to "heel."

Lead from the side at the base of the neck.

A trainer once told me he wanted the horse to walk well behind him, and that coming closer was "disrespect." My belief is that no disrespect is involved if the horse walks where you want him. And, I've led enough stallions toward mares to realize what happens if a horse with a long lead runs in front of you—should he kick back in an attempt to get free, the kicks will likely be aimed (deliberately or not) right at your chest. Also, a horse walking behind me is one I can't see, and if I can't see him, I can't pick up on his body language.

That said, walking single file is necessary on a ledge trail or a tight path lined with trees. Your horse should be well trained enough to do as you wish, and in this case that means walking behind you as you lead. Most horses sense this change easily enough and refrain from pushing up beside you in narrow quarters.

When leading there's a temptation to wrap the lead rope around your hand for better leverage. Don't do it! In all aspects of horsemanship, avoid anything that inadvertently ties you to the horse. In a spook situation a lead rope around your hand can become a half hitch, and you can be dragged. Instead, simply double the rope so that you're holding on to two strands of the rope without wrapping. That gives a more solid purchase, especially with a large-diameter lead.

Concern about becoming inadvertently tied to the horses should be ever-present when handling them. With me, this concern is almost phobic, and I do everything possible to avoid any situation likely to cause it. While riding, the first and most obvious worry, and rightly so, is that of becoming hung up in a stirrup after a "wreck," whether from being bucked off or falling. Gruesome stories abound of riders being hurt or killed after being dragged on the ground by a foot that's managed to slip all the way through a stirrup.

The "school solution" for such a situation is to turn over on your belly while being dragged, the theory being that your foot will more likely come free in the inverted position. Or, your boot will be more likely to slip off your foot when inverted. We must all hope we'll never have the "opportunity" to test this theory. Prevention is a far better route.

On a ride in Spain, our guide, a tough British woman, no doubt wishing to see what sort of riders she'd contracted for the coming week, started our horseback experience with, "Canter on," her command to let the horses have their heads on a hard-packed gravel road. Although my seat felt fine as I got with the rhythm of the hard-muscled gelding I'd been assigned, I was immediately aware that the stirrups on the English cavalry saddle were too tight to release my feet easily should a wreck occur. It became evident that the guide's idea of a canter was instead a flat-out gallop, which made for some anxious moments until the rest stop, when I was able to swap stirrups with a smaller rider.

Usually, however, the worry is that a foot can go entirely through the stirrup during a mishap, hanging up the rider. The best solution is using a set of tapaderos, "taps," stirrup covers of the sort that absolutely prevent a foot from sliding all the way through. Avoid the type with no floor, because they could make the situation even worse. You want a tapadero that is completely enclosed. Then, avoid boots that have an aggressive traction sole. A little traction pattern is fine and helps prevent your foot from inadvertently sliding out of the stirrup, but too much in the way of traction lugs and it's easy for your foot to become hung up as you dismount.

Fully enclosed tapadero.

And yes, wear *boots*. I see all sorts of footwear on riders, but the traditional cowboy boot, or something similar from a different culture, is still one of the safest types of footwear. The narrow toe helps your foot find its way easily into the stirrup, while the prominent heel helps prevent insertion too far into it. The high leather uppers protect your calf from bruising against the stirrup leathers.

Popular in the mountains I frequent are packer boots, lace-up boots with a narrow toe and substantial heel. They're designed to make a packer's work on the ground a bit more comfortable than a straight cowboy boot, while having some of the same advantages when riding. I use them while

Traditional western boot and packer boot.

packing autumn hunting camps, but with this caution—should you become hung up in the stirrup and dragged, this type of boot will not come off your foot, potentially saving you. Use them with tapaderos!

While riding, a good rule of thumb is to avoid loops of all kinds. The seasoned cowboy who ropes cattle must have a lariat rope coiled and ready, but unless you're a roper, avoid anything on your saddle that could conceivably catch an arm or leg during a wreck. An extra-long latigo that hung toward the ground was pronounced to be just fine by my father-in-law when I expressed concern about it. "It's okay, Dan," he said, "because it doesn't make a loop." He stopped me from tying its loose end back up on the saddle— it was safer hanging with its end toward the ground because, as Elmer said, it wouldn't catch on anything that way.

So what does this principle say about the *mecate* (sometimes corrupted to "McCarthy") that most trainers recommend today? We're talking about the rope coming from the hackamore or snaffle bit that riders tuck into their belts while riding. In the old California style of horsemanship, the *mecate* was used to adjust the bosal, but now clinicians encourage its use with snaffle bits, and yes, it's handy for quickly tying one's horse. In theory, tucking a *mecate* into your belt helps keep your horse from running off should you be bucked off, that is, if you are fortunate enough to be intact after the incident.

But putting it bluntly, in the backcountry a *mecate* tucked into your belt is just another rope that can hang you. Why modern clinicians encourage its use is beyond me. While riding, this additional rope looping down to the horse's nose begs to catch itself on brush, and in a wreck it can easily entangle a foot or an arm.

One of the worst reasons for using a *mecate* is that is somehow makes you into a traditional, authentic cowboy. Peruse the hundreds of photographs taken by frontier photographer L. A. Huffman of cowboys in the Dakotas and Montana, men who'd come to the "Big Open"—as we sometimes call the endless sagebrush country of the West—with cattle herds from Texas and Mexico, and you'll be hard-pressed to spot a *mecate*.

You will see in these photos what was called a "graze rope," a long rope attached to the horse's halter (worn under the bridle) then coiled and attached to the pommel of the saddle like a lariat rope. Every hour or two the cowboy would dismount, roll a cigarette, squat in the resting position that only works for slim, in-shape human beings, and shake out the graze rope. His horse could then snatch bits of prairie grass while the cowboy took his break.

Becoming entangled with a thousand-pound animal with the potential to spook, then drag you over hill and dale, is a scenario to prevent at all costs, and it can develop in unexpected ways. Many years ago, while off my horse to open a gate, a strange thing happened. Taking a break and eyeballing my alfalfa field, hoping for a good stand of hay, I felt my right leg strangely rise from an unseen force behind me. It happened more quickly than I can tell it, but my leg kept rising, threatening to topple me, allowing only a quick glance over my shoulder to see the whites of my gelding's eyes. I'm sure he saw mine as well!

Rockytop was three years old, more than sixteen hands tall, and very spirited. His head was in the air, his manner telegraphing "I'm ready to bolt." Just short of the point when standing on one leg would have grown impossible, my boot let go. Had it not, I'd been dragged by a tall horse, my body at the mercy of his front feet.

The incident was caused by a freak situation you probably couldn't duplicate if you tried. I was wearing spurs. As Rockytop grazed next to my heel, the rowel of my right spur slipped through the ring of his bit. Startled, he had raised his head, my boot coming with it, his panic increasing (along with mine) the higher my leg followed his bit. The gelding's natural resistance to the pull panicked him all the more. Thankfully, the rowel came loose at the critical moment. But the story illustrates the old principle, "If something can go wrong, it will go wrong, and sometimes in a way you'd never expect."

We'll touch on safety frequently in coming chapters, including the precautions that should accompany all interaction with horses. The last thing the referee says to boxers before the bell rings to start the match, "Protect yourself at all times," applies equally well to all dimensions of horsemanship.

CHAPTER THREE

FOUNDATION TRAINING FOR THE BACKCOUNTRY HORSE

Many of us in the horse world are guilty of allowing our animals to get into a particular groove, then failing to expand their horizons. As a rancher I've been guilty of this. Training a horse "on the job" is fine, but it sometimes leaves gaps. I rode my gelding, Partner, for years in a particular valley that featured a small braided stream with many crossings. None of them were large enough to justify a bridge—the creek could always be easily forded—and Partner was accustomed to driveway bridges and small creek bridges on our ranch. Similarly, he'd many times crossed a small training bridge within our arena.

But it had been many years since I'd ridden in areas that featured long trail bridges over large streams, and when I'd frequented those areas it had been while riding other horses. I'd forgotten that fact. On a chilly morning, with two packhorses in tow carrying trail-building materials for the Forest Service, I came to a long bridge over a rapid river, its planks covered with slick white frost. Partner refused to cross. The packhorses I was ponying precluded the assertive action I might have taken if I'd been riding unladen. I was perplexed and embarrassed, but I waved another rider past me. Partner then consented to cross the bridge behind the other horse.

Perhaps some gaps in training are nearly impossible to avoid, but before we head for the backcountry we should eliminate as many as possible. Unfortunately, this is where so many weekend clinics fall short. Too often, perhaps to impress clients, the clinician starts an untrained animal and rides it successfully in a relatively short time in front of an admiring audience. But in too many cases what's really happened is that he has overwhelmed

A bridge over white water.

the animal with stimuli and achieved a brief cooperation. Could he turn the horse out for a week, catch him, then ride to the hills? The horse has received surface training comparable to a human memorizing a series of five or six numbers in a few seconds so that you can recite them back to another individual. But will you remember them next week?

Good training involves hard work and repetition, and if training looks easy, it's probably of the surface type. Can it be counted on when you're on a ledge trail in the mountains and lightning begins to crack or when the horse ahead of you or behind you blows its cork?

When I was a horse-crazy town kid, I sat on a pole fence to watch an old cowboy trainer work with a stocky black stallion. The trainer's son had told me a session would take place, and I'd shown up eager to see some sort of rodeo. I was sorely disappointed. I watched for a solid half hour while the old cowboy repeated just one thing endlessly. Standing next to the horse he grasped the left stirrup as if to mount, then thrust it downward, not very hard, just smartly enough to make a slapping noise. The horse didn't really spook, just started slightly. But the trainer kept doing it, over and over, each time drawing less reaction from the horse. But as long as the horse moved, the man repeated the action. Finally, the horse stood completely still, ignoring the movement and sound, and then the training session was over. I hadn't seen what I came to see, but I believe I learned something.

It's unlikely a clinician would have gone through such a process in front of an impatient audience. Wanting to show them progress, he'd possibly have tolerated an incomplete result so that he could move on, perhaps even mounting the horse long before it was truly ready.

Additionally, weekend clinicians rarely emphasize skills that are crucial for horse use in the backcountry. Unfortunately, instructors themselves are often not well-versed in skills I consider essential. A good friend from the East, in preparation for a horseback hunt in the Rockies, wisely arranged for riding lessons. He afterward praised the instructor and felt that the process was very worthwhile. However, in asking about proper rigging of a highline in camp my friend discovered that his instructor had never heard of a highline and had no idea how to rig one. Although an excellent teacher of equitation, backcountry knowledge was in a different sphere.

In this chapter we'll look at those gaps that might be present in a horse that's already trained. What bits of knowledge and awareness should this horse possess before being considered a safe backcountry animal but that might have been skipped or overlooked in his basic training? Obviously, everything mentioned can (and should) be included in the "boot camp" of a colt in training, but we're assuming that may not have been the case.

FEET, ROPES, AND TIES

Let's start with the feet. Any trained horse should allow his feet to be handled, picked up, and probably shod. But I've seen trained horses that freaked when first hobbled. To prevent that and to create an animal that can be restrained in the backcountry, we need to go a step or two beyond that elementary knowledge, to back up to basics.

We teach all our colts to lead by each foot. It's easier than it sounds, and a horse is never too old to learn it. I normally start with the left front foot. Keeping the halter lead rope in place, I either tie a soft cotton rope around the pastern or I use a hobble half, which is a bit better. I don't attempt at first to lead only with the foot. I hold both the lead rope and the cotton rope, putting a bit of pressure on both as I go forward. Since he's been taught to lead from the halter, the horse normally does not object.

Start by leading with both lead rope and rope to front foot.

From there I gradually progress to the other feet. It's surprising how quickly most horses learn this. After a bit of practice, still working in a small corral or enclosure, you can eliminate the lead rope on the halter completely, though you'll probably want to keep it in place for the first session on each foot, particularly the hind ones. It's best to avoid putting much pressure on the horse's foot. Usually just holding the rope firmly is enough, letting the horse create slack when he steps in the right direction, then tightening the rope again. Creating the slack is his reward for coming in the right direction. Knowledge seems to transfer from one foot to the others, and usually each successive foot, including the hind ones, is easier.

Through this process the horse learns to give to pressure on the foot, and not only when a human grasps it to lift for trimming. Now the horse understands that the rope or hobble half means restraint and that he must give to its pressure. You've not only laid the groundwork for hobbling and

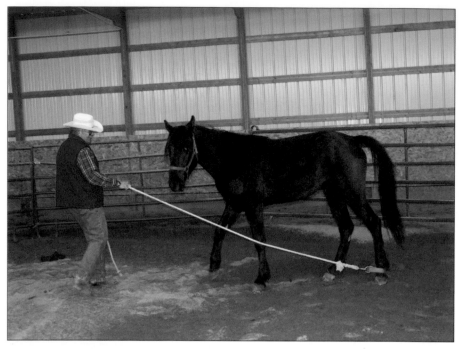

Progress to all four feet.

picketing; you've created a safer horse, one less likely to hurt himself should he be caught in wire.

Tying up a hind foot is a logical extension of this routine, one which every horse should accept (but too few are taught). Although it's often used to limit a horse's motion during training, for instance when the animal is first being saddled or, in the case of a packhorse, asked to accept panniers, gradual, patient preparation is a better approach to those tasks. Nonetheless, a horse's acceptance of one foot being tied up is invaluable, particularly in a dicey backcountry situation. Treating a painful wound or pulling porcupine quills, when no sedatives are available, challenges even the gentlest, most well-trained horse. Few can be expected to stand still during such a situation.

Tying up a hind foot will limit unwanted motion during an emergency, though it certainly won't preclude it completely. I start with a rope around thirty feet long, of cotton if possible, though harsher ropes may be used when you have a hobble half available for the hind pastern. Tie one end of the rope around the base of the horse's neck with a bowline. Yes, a

Ouch! Removing porcupine quills is likely to take either sedation or restraint such as tying up a foot.

bowline, no other knot, and if you don't know how to tie one, now's the time to learn. There's no more important knot for the horseman or the sailor. It's so revered that I recently ran into a fifty-nine-page treatise on the bowline and its variations. The knot section of this book, chapter 14, will show you how to tie it.

The bowline absolutely will not tighten under stress, a safety must for a rope that will encircle the horse's neck. And, if it's stressed, you can always get it untied.

From the bowline loop, feed the rest of the rope back and between the horse's hind legs, letting it fall down behind one hind hoof. If you're using a hobble half, run the rope through the ring on the hobble. Otherwise, just keep it placed around the horse's pastern.

Now bring the end of the rope back up and through the circle made by the bowline at the base of the animal's neck. You now have a sort of block-and-tackle, two-to-one mechanical advantage for raising the horse's hind foot. Go slowly at first. From his lessons in leading by each foot, the horse has learned to yield to a pull, but this is a bit different. Gradually increase the pull until you raise the foot, giving whatever verbal command you use when doing farrier work. (I simply use the word "foot!")

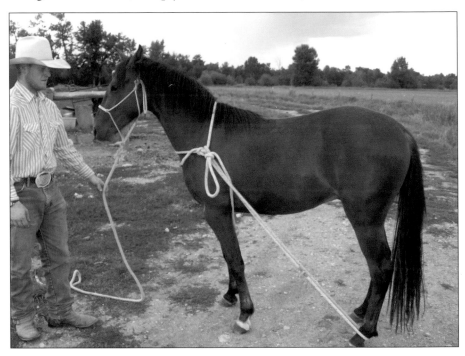

Trainer Travis Young tying up a hind foot.

When the horse allows you to raise its foot above the ground with the rope and when you've repeated the process several times, quickly tie off the end you're holding to the standing part of the rope (the part coming up from the hind foot). I use a slipped half hitch for the purpose, another handy knot to learn and one that's illustrated in the knot section. The quick-release tie-up, a knot I tend to favor, also works well. Because some horses struggle at this point, it's important to never tie a horse up with a halter and lead rope during this process. If a tied horse struggles with a foot tied up, it can fall, and hampered from catching itself correctly because of the tied foot, injure itself.

Don't leave the horse for long after tying up the foot. Keep it under a minute; then turn the bowline loop around to the other side, and tie up the other hind foot. Teaching a horse to accept this restraint may well cut down on the trauma involved when you really need to limit his motion.

It's only after these lessons, leading by each foot and tying up hind feet, that we move on to hobbling. No matter how carefully you've prepared the horse with the process above, it's still important to first hobble in a safe, soft place. A sandy corral or arena is ideal, but make sure there's plenty of room. Some horses will initially fight the hobbles, and they can be awkward in doing so. You don't want a horse to fall into a fence or other obstruction.

More often, though, the horse that's been properly prepared will stand completely still or will gently test his restraints by lifting one foot, then the other. But always avoid being directly in front of the horse, lest he be the type

Two types of hobbles.

that quickly learns to cover ground by raising both front feet and taking a forward hop.

Hobbles come in several types. The simplest and lightest consist of a strap with two rings and a buckle. The hobble encircles one pastern, goes through the first ring, then through the second ring and around the other pastern, where it buckles. This type is handy, but if made of nylon can chafe an animal that struggles. The same configuration of leather or of a synthetic lined with padding is somewhat kinder to the horse.

Another type consists of two hobble halves connected by a short chain or strap. These normally allow a bit more freedom, but that can come at a cost with a horse that really learns to move in them.

Work from the side while hobbling.

Applying hobbles, especially to a horse not used to them, requires care. If you've prepared as I've outlined above, by teaching the horse to lead by each foot, then he'll be used to your attaching an item to his pastern. As always, work from the horse's shoulder, starting on the near (left) side, not in front of him. If you're agile enough to attach the hobble to the near pastern by bending down or crouching, that's best. If you must kneel to attach it, just be all the more careful, because in that position you've lost the ability to move quickly.

After you've attached the hobble to the first pastern, slide the other half of the hobble toward the off pastern. With a seasoned horse in which you're very confident, you might reach across and attach the hobble to the off pastern, but with a horse unused to the process it's better to move to the off side and attach the second half the of the hobble. If this is your animal's first time, or if your seasoned horse is anxious to move forward into grass, work quickly and deftly to attach to the second pastern. It's at this last moment of attachment the horse is likely to jump, pinching your fingers.

Throughout the process it's best to keep the horse's halter and lead rope in place, taking a bit of slack out of the lead so that the horse knows it's

Hobble on the pasterns, not the cannon bones.

restrained. Then, remove the halter so that the horse is less likely to become snagged, or perhaps to catch a hind foot on it.

Notice I continually mention the pastern as the proper place to attach hobbles. Yes, you'll see photos in tack catalogs and in magazines of hobbles placed up on the front cannon bones. Don't do it. The cannon bone does not flex. Tendons in the cannon are right against the bone, with no protection but the horse's hide. Pasterns, on the other hand, are designed to flex. That said, there's no point of attachment in horse restraint that is 100 percent safe—accidents can and do happen, but careful preparation will help prevent them.

Even with the preparation we've outlined, there's no sure way of predicting what will happen when the horse discovers his two front feet are fastened together. Be ready for a little lively stuff, the reason for soft footing and plenty of room in the area you choose. I've never had a horse hurt himself while learning about hobbles, but I've had a few go down to their knees, while others struggle to pull one foot away from the other. Soft, padded hobbles are best for this, and rest assured, the struggle won't last long. Horses fear falling, and most soon learn to cooperate with the device, often by taking baby steps.

Some, though, learn too well. I have horses that can literally run while hobbled, and many can move along with giant hops, keeping their front feet together, dangerous if you happen to be in front of them. I once owned a walking horse colt that could jump fences while hobbled. We repeatedly found him on the wrong side of a paddock fence where he'd been hobbled to graze and finally caught him in the act. He'd stand facing the fence, rise with both front feet synchronized, then leap.

Because many soon become so adept at moving while hobbled, I never hobble all my horses while in camp. I keep a good reliable saddle horse tied, waiting until later for his chance to graze. The alternative might be a long walk to the trailhead.

For horses that move extremely well with regular hobbles, the three-legged type can be the answer. These feature a strap that runs from the ring at the middle of the front hobble between the horse's front feet, back to a hobble half on one of its hind pasterns. Three-legged hobbles tend to befuddle even the best hobble athletes, because they take away the animal's ability to hop. The horse will learn to move forward and graze with small steps, but he won't head over the ridge or down the trail.

Three-legged hobbles limit movement.

Just as leading by feet prepares a horse for hobbling, hobbling prepares a horse for the method of picketing we favor in the backcountry. Both hobbling and picketing allow grazing, a plus in the backcountry since it can reduce the amount of feed to be packed in. But be aware that some areas of public land don't allow grazing.

We picket with a hobble half attached to one front foot, the safest way we've found. We never picket with a line to the halter because it is a dangerous practice. A foot can easily become entangled in the halter, and the head of the horse is the last place you'd want to see the horse take a jolt should a real spook, such as a bear walking through camp, occur.

We also don't picket from a hind foot. A horse's hind limbs contain the complex and easily injured stifle joint, and a direct, hard pull can result an injury for life. As we've said, any restraint method, given the worst scenario, can result in injury, but over time the front-foot picket, attached to the pastern, has proven safest.

In addition to a hobble half, you'll need a rope around thirty feet in length. If possible, it should be of a soft material to avoid chafe. Cotton works well, but is not particularly strong or long-lived. Some soft-weave synthetics are better choices. Some sort of swivel in the line is essential. Otherwise, the restless horse, foraging for grass, will unwind a twist-strand rope and ruin it. Actually, using two, a swivel at the point of attachment to the hobble half, plus one on the other end of the rope where it attaches to the picket stake, is a good idea.

All the steps outlined above—leading by the foot, tying up a foot, and hobbling—serve as training for picketing by a front foot. Even so, be careful the first time. Before releasing the picketed horse, I always lead him out to the end of the picket rope so that he feels the restraint and is aware it's there. Otherwise, thinking he's free when I remove the halter, he may run off quickly and hit the end of the rope too hard. And yes, it's best to remove the halter when picketing a horse.

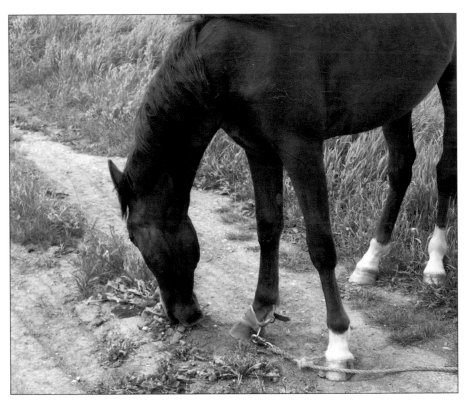

Picket by a front pastern after horse is thoroughly accustomed to hobbling.

Restraint by the foot through the steps we've outlined, leading to picketing, makes for a horse less likely to hurt himself if caught by the foot. A horse so trained is also likely to result in a happier farrier, and this training allows restraint in camp through hobbling and picketing. But some restraint comes via the halter, of course, and we've assumed a trained horse leads easily and ties with a lead rope. But it's not quite that simple. Some horses pull back, and some horse owners do not tie their horses correctly or with a knot that stays put, yet allows easy untying. A review is in order.

We halterbreak foals early in the game, first using a rump rope together with the halter's lead rope to minimize pressure on the foal's neck. I try not to pull directly forward, instead going slightly to the side and simply putting on modest amount of pressure on the ropes. Soon the foal figures out that he can remove the pressure by moving the direction you wish. Thus begins a basic principle of horse training, pressure/release.

At some point, though, the young horse must learn that he's not to pull back and that doing so will not result in freedom. When he's a bit more mature, perhaps as a yearling, he must be tied relatively short with a halter

At some point after a colt is halterbroke we tie them under supervision fairly high and short to something they cannot break.

and lead rope he can't break to an equally unbreakable post. There's no way around this. He should be tied no lower than natural nose level and watched closely. Some horses readily accept this, while others put up a bit of a struggle, but it's essential nonetheless. Should the horse ever learn that a tussle while tied will result in breaking loose, he may become a horse that's impossible to hold without injuring himself.

I once owned a powerful Quarter Horse mare that had been spoiled in this fashion. Rosie was gentle in all other respects, but would throw a tantrum if you attempted to tie her. Since we bought her at a sale we had no idea how she'd become that way, but our first attempts at tying resulted in broken halters, posts, and lead ropes. She was calculating in her routine. Tie her and she'd stand still for a moment, then throw her entire 1,100 pounds straight back while letting out a squeal for good measure.

Some trainers have routines in their bags of tricks which they claim can cure such a horse, but none are certain or very easy on the horse. Elmer and I attempted to cure her just once, using a nylon rope no horse could break, a bowline around her neck (the only safe knot for the purpose), tied to the strongest post on the ranch. Her attempts to break it were so extreme that my father-in-law slipped in through the dust and cut the rope—he couldn't stand watching her further punishing herself and feared she'd pull muscles or worse.

What about "breakaway" systems designed to give way when the horse pulls back, ostensibly to prevent injury? Frankly, they've been designed by folks who flunked Psychology 101. A tie system that breaks under pressure in effect trains the horse to pull back. Perhaps his first release will be inadvertent, after a spook. But he's rewarded when he breaks loose with a bite of grass or the freedom to run. Next time he'll try harder.

Even into maturity it's important that horses be tied fairly high so they can't reach the ground to graze, quite short, with a strong halter and lead rope fastened to something solid. In the wide-open American West, loss of one's saddle horse can create a survival situation. The old-timers' saying, "Better to count ribs than tracks" reflects a reality recognized by cowboys and mountain men. Given a choice, they'd have rather deprived their horses of feed through the night than see only the tracks of their escaped animals in the morning, and be left to face a grim situation.

Bridle reins are not for tying. The type I favor for the feel they give my rein hand are relatively slim leather, not overly strong. Also, anything attached solidly to the bit will transmit unwanted shock to the mouth of a horse should he pull back during a spook, perhaps with damage. We favor riding with a halter under the bridle for our backcountry travel. For short stops we tie the reins to our saddle horns with two facing half hitches, tying the horse with lead ropes we carry on our saddles. For longer stops we remove the bridle and bit so the horse will be more comfortable during his wait.

Attend a gathering of many horses and riders and you'll eventually see someone's saddle horse walking around loose, dragging his lead rope. Often the cause is an inappropriate knot used to secure the animal. I've seen all sorts of knots used, but to fit my criteria a tie-up knot should be quick to tie, strong, and easy to untie, even if it's been subjected to some pressure. The quick-release knot illustrated in chapter 14 works well, but others can be useful, too.

Of course, horses can break loose from causes other than improper knots. Lead ropes that attach to the halter with a swivel snap are handy, but snaps can fail. Swivels with a sliding latch are often weak and can freeze during cold weather. "Panic snaps" are strong, but should be kept lubricated so that the sliding section that locks the two hooks engages fully. "Bull snaps" are quite strong, though I've seen some that are poorly made.

Strongest of all are systems that completely eliminate hardware on both the lead rope and halter. Nylon rope halters knotted to lead ropes are strongest, but must be properly tied. The downside is lack of a swivel. Tie your horse to a loop on a highline without a swivel and you may find a ruined lead rope in the morning, twisted beyond recognition by the horse's constant circling.

And it's the highline that has emerged as the most acceptable system for retaining horses in the backcountry. Your picketed or hobbled horse mustn't be left that way during the night for his safety and yours. When closer control is necessary, the highline is relatively safe and if set up on high, rocky ground, less destructive to the environment. (Some repair with the camp shovel will likely be necessary when leaving the area.)

We'll discuss rigging the highline in camp later in this book. But for training purposes it's wise to rig an overhead line of strong half-inch rope around home to check whether your horse is bothered by an overhead tie. I've never actually encountered an animal that seemed to sense much difference, but a strong highline mock-up is a good test. Keep the line well above the horse's ears and tie a picket-line loop in its middle. Tie your horse to this, but watch him. Keep the tie short enough that he can't reach the ground to graze. If the horse is well halterbroke and used to tying without pulling back, you likely won't have an issue.

GETTING HIM USED TO BELLS AND WHISTLES: "DESENSITIZATION" VERSUS "SACKING OUT"

Since horse training began humans have looked for ways to overcome a horse's natural desire to escape a situation he considers dangerous. Much of horse training consists of this very thing—creating a useful animal that will not flee at the slightest provocation. Your horse may be well trained for what he's used to doing, but still not be safe for some of the situations you'll tackle in the backcountry.

The traditional approach to this dilemma was "sacking out." There are other terms for it, no doubt, and most trainers still use it to a degree. I've mentioned watching as a boy while a trainer slapped a stirrup leather against the horse in a relatively gentle manner, continuing at length until the horse finally quit reacting. That trainer was quite gentle in this process, and very patient.

Some version of sacking out was once considered absolutely necessary in the training process. The trainer would swing the saddle blanket (or an empty grain sack) onto the horse's back, do it repeatedly from both sides, and refuse to quit until the horse accepted the action without a negative response. Then it was on to the next step.

But I've noticed that the era of the weekend clinic doesn't always include much of this process. The need to be slow and patient, to take time until the horse really accepts what's happening, doesn't always fit with pleasing a paying audience. Sometimes horses are buffaloed, in a sense bullied by the new surroundings, and like the deer in the headlights, "cooperate." But there will be a reckoning someday, when the shortcomings of the horse's training come to the fore, and you don't want it to occur on a mountain trail.

The old cowboys were guilty of some of the same shortcomings as trainers. Theodore Roosevelt told of how horses were made ready for a cowboy's remuda, normally consisting of ten horses. A man called the "horse breaker" would come around from ranch to ranch. While others held the horse, he would saddle it, bridle it, and get on to "buck it out." After four or five rides the horse was deemed ready for use. The cowboy took over.

Such horses were not truly trained, of course, and Roosevelt had one go over backward on him. He was lucky to escape with a broken collarbone. He was bucked off many times as well.

But here's the difference between then and now: Then the average cowboy was a slim, tough-as-nails young man who could practically ride a comet. His remuda became trained on the job with risks neither you nor I wish to take, and he was physically up to the job. On one cattle-driving experience, stopping a stampede, Roosevelt mentioned that while galloping headlong over coulees and ridges not a single one of his group escaped going end over end at least once.

It's easy to criticize such a tough version of horse training, but it was born of necessity. Horses were cheap, training was expensive, and the animals were needed now, not after months of gentle training. But even under these circumstances people recognized there was a better way. Theodore Roosevelt, in one of his musings, looked forward to a winter in his log house during which he could read and write (he was a ravenous reader and an incredibly prolific writer) but also to break two special colts he's kept for himself. He said he wished to do it the slow way, the gentle way, and asserted that the end result would be a better horse.

In recent years the term desensitization has become popular. Frankly, I don't care for it. The word implies a numbing of the senses, a sensual "dumbing down," even if that's not the intended meaning. We aren't drugging the animal or decreasing the acuteness of its wonderful senses. Rather, we wish to keep the horse's senses of sight, scent, touch, and hearing, in so many ways superior to our own, fully intact. But we want a horse that while aware, is also tolerant. This will come with trust, but it takes time.

The "sacking out" approach can certainly work, but it has pitfalls. Similar to what psychologists call "flooding," sacking out involves continuing a frightening stimuli until the horse decides it's not going to hurt him. You swing the blanket onto his back, do it over and over again, and normally he'll eventually stop reacting. But what if he doesn't? What if dinnertime comes and goes and you've made no progress?

I used to think it was absolutely necessary to stick with the stimuli no matter how long it took. As the years passed, I modified this belief. Yes, I think it's best to carry through until the horse completely tolerates the stimuli, but I don't think all is lost if the session is interrupted. I've worked with colts that seem to pick up where I left off and progress from there.

In any case, the backcountry horse needs a more thorough education in various stimuli than those in some other disciplines, because he's going to be asked to do such a variety of things. I've always discouraged folks from saying their mounts are "just trail horses." Truly, the trail horse, and particularly the one slated for wilderness adventures, must be the ultimate equine generalist. Competency in just one area of discipline is not enough. On the trail, backcountry horses can encounter a variety of different obstacles including moose, bogs, rocky ledges, and llamas, perhaps while carrying bulky cargo on his back. And, on some remote trails he's likely to meet a backcountry bicycle hurtling down the trail toward him.

The bicycle, so nearly silent, can present one of the more dangerous encounters on the trail, and there's an increasing push to allow them within wilderness areas. In 2017, a bill was introduced on the floor of Congress to amend the Wilderness Act and allow bicycles in wilderness areas. I shudder when I think of the consequences possible when a speeding bicycle meets a pack train on a ledge trail. Expose your horse to bicycles as frequently as possible under controlled conditions.

A friend of mine once won a world championship in a gaited horse show. He told me that before he entered the ring, he was sure one of two things would happen. It was fifty-fifty, he said. Either he would win the class or he'd be bucked off. The horse was scarcely broke, but if he could keep it going in the right direction in its magnificent gaits, he'd probably be okay. If not, my friend would likely hit the arena sand. Such specialization can't work for our equine generalists as they negotiate the backcountry. A horse such as this would be useless and dangerous.

Foundation training of the backcountry horse needs to include the sort of equipment we'll use. (What we encounter while riding the horse will be the subject of the next chapter.) I'm a great believer in "try it at home, first."

Don't wait for the trailhead to try a different saddle, saddlebags, a crupper, and so on for the first time.

I was bequeathed an English flat saddle years ago, and it sat in my tack shed for months before I finally decided to give it a try. I saddled Major, my most reliable gelding, and looked forward to a new experience. I got one! Major paused after I mounted, snorted, and then gave me the only bucks of his entire career. This wasn't serious bucking, more the sort we westerners call "kicking up," but they did get my attention. The saddle seemed to fit properly, and one would have thought Major would be relieved to carry a twenty-pound saddle rather that a thirty-five-pound one, but that wasn't the case. It looked different, felt different, and probably smelled different from the one he was used to.

Similarly, the average western saddle is quite an extensive affair, perhaps employing a second (rear) cinch, a breast collar, and maybe a crupper. Yes, we can say that the truly well-trained horse should be bothered by none of this, but we're looking for "holes" in his training, and we want to discover them sooner rather than later. If your horse is only used to a flat saddle, prepare by saddling and riding (at home) with the one you'll be using in the backcountry.

The breast collar isn't likely to create a bothersome new sensation, but that can't be said of a rear cinch, particularly if used properly, that is cinched snugly, not allowed to hang where a fly-seeking rear hoof or a branch on the trail could catch it. A horse that's only felt a cinch on the middle or front part of his rib cage just might object. Take the precaution of leading the horse around wearing his new tack, circle him, maybe longe him in a circle before getting on. Let the rear cinch hang a little loose for the first ride, then take up the slack.

The crupper is more problematic. I'd like to see cruppers in more general use among backcountry riders. In Spain, they were standard equipment on mountain saddles worn by both horses and mules. Horses learn to tuck their tails tightly against the crupper on downhill grades, helping to hold the saddle back.

Even if you don't use a crupper, it's important to accustom the backcountry horse to it or at least to something like it that fits under the tail. If your horse will ever be packed he'll be fitted with a breeching (sometimes pronounced "britchin'"). And, if he's ever to pony (lead) pack animals,

In Spain Emily leads Paciencia, an Andalusian mare, equipped with a crupper, standard equipment in this area.

eventually a lead rope will work its way up under his tail. Better that he experience the sensation up front, not on a mountain trail.

Start by making sure your horse is accustomed to his tail being handled. Obviously, this should have been accomplished through grooming or tail trimming, but we're going to ask for more. A soft cotton rope passed under the tail is a good start. Gently pass it under the tail, grasping both ends so that it loops under the tail, then lift just enough to make contact with the underside of the tail. Stay to the side of the horse's rump while doing this. Although it may seem mares would be more sensitive than geldings to this process, I haven't found that necessarily so.

Adjust the crupper a bit on the loose side at first, but not so that it hangs. Again, move it up and down and side to side from the ground, working at the horse's side. You'll soon discover whether the horse is particularly sensitive to the crupper, but that won't tell you for sure how the horse will react to the tighter sensation likely when you descend a steep grade. Ride on more level ground for a bit before tackling mountain descents with the crupper in place.

I saw a trainer prepare a horse to handle a crupper by riding the mare while holding a loop of cotton rope up under her tail. The trainer took the mare in all gaits, neck reining with one hand, holding the rope in the other. That's a bit on the aggressive side, perhaps, but it did the job.

Saddlebags, raincoats, saddle scabbards, canteens hanging on the horn—all such present new sensations to the horse. His rearward vision will spot awkward items tied behind the saddle; he'll hear water sloshing in your canteen and the flapping sound the wind makes on your raincoat tied to the saddle. You must remember that this big animal is so sensitive he feels a fly touch his pastern. Yes, we can say that the well-trained saddle horse should be beyond any concerns with accessories mounted on the saddle. But let's not assume this—testing your horse's reaction to the equipment you'll use on the trail in the safety of your home corral or arena is always a good idea.

A friend bought a young horse that he considered reasonably well trained. Planning for a hunting trip, it never occurred to him that this responsive horse, tuned to key off leg cues, would be bothered by a saddle scabbard hanging diagonally on the left side of his saddle, the barrel end of the scabbard low and under the stirrup leather. He took the horse to a trailhead, giving him his first experience with the scabbard in new, scary

Elmer Johnson, the author's father-in-law and mentor.

surroundings, where horses were saddled in darkness by the light of head-lamps.

My friend placed his toe in the stirrup and began to mount, but didn't get far. The horse, feeling the saddle scabbard press into his side, reacted to what he interpreted as a massive leg cue. He took off like a rocket. My friend, luckily not hurt, but having no taste for conflict with a horse under dicey circumstances, borrowed another mount. Chagrined, he admitted that trying out his gear at home under controlled circumstances would likely have prevented the incident.

The approach I recommend is an easy and gentle version of the old-timers' "sacking out." Expose, rub, pet, and generally let the horse discover through your patience that these new objects won't hurt him. Swing your rolled-up raincoat onto the back of the saddle, do it gently but firmly, and if you get a reaction, do it again. And again, and again, if necessary. Then do it from the other side.

Don't be overly tentative. You're the horse's leader, and he needs to know you are there. Touch and action should be firm and decisive, not light and flitting. Helping my father-in-law irrigate, I needed to tie a wet, rolled-up canvas tarp onto the back of my mare. "Just slap it up there, Dan," he said, "Don't be sneaky about it. If she jumps, she jumps, but she'll get used to it." He turned out to be right. It took several times, but then all was well.

And through it all remember that horses are individuals. What one quickly accepted, another may not. A favorite gelding of mine detested the sound of Velcro parting. He's the only horse I've owned that paid it much mind, and he did it to his dying day. I could have spent a day opening my jacket, flooding him with the stimuli, the grating sound, and maybe I should have. But since his response was not dangerous, I found his aversion for the sound rather amusing and decided I could allow him that one little indulgence.

But for your future safety, be persistent. And always, always, try it first at home.

CHAPTER FOUR

BASIC TRAIL TRAINING FOR HORSE AND RIDER

TACKING UP AND MOUNTING

So let's back up a bit, to basic safety for tacking up and riding. We'll touch on these issues again as the book progresses, because as humans, we're all fallible—we need constant reminders. We'll focus on western tack, the type the majority of readers are likely to use in the backcountry, but the principles apply universally; all sorts of tack can work. I've ridden in Iceland where people ride the rugged backcountry in what we Montanans would consider "English" saddles, and herd livestock with them as well.

But the traditional western saddle evolved out of need for a stout (and unfortunately heavy) structure for riding that allowed rugged living on horseback. A horn was needed for roping or dallying (wrapping) the lead rope of a recalcitrant pack animal. Saddle strings allowed for tying on gear. The deep seat helped the rider stay aboard over hill and dale in rough country.

Of course, there are other suitable saddles. Plantation saddles are often used by folks who follow dogs in field trials, and most feature D-rings to facilitate tying on accessories and saddle scabbards. But they do lack a horn.

Western saddles vary widely, but most will have the basic components seen in the illustration, except, perhaps, the tapaderos. Prudent backcountry riders will add these. An internet search will turn up a number of suppliers. Just remember to prescribe the type that fully encloses the foot, not those with an open bottom.

Early western saddles (until approximately 1900) were all slick-forked, sometimes called A-forked, with pommels that tapered up toward the horn.

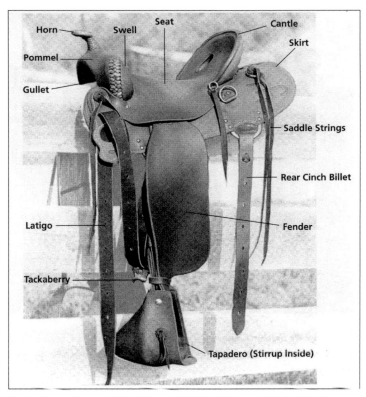

Parts of a western saddle, this one by Rick Ericksen of Ennis, Montana. Note holes in cantle, which allow basket hitching load to the saddle in a pinch.

Swells (sometimes called bulges) became popular in the twentieth century, and are designed to help you stay mounted should the horse buck. Slick-forked saddles are comfortable and have again become popular, sometimes with padded add-on bucking rolls. I've never personally understood why you'd want an Λ fork saddle if you felt the need for bucking rolls, but each to his own.

Early saddles usually had just one cinch, placed a bit back from the front legs in what was called the three-quarter position or even well back, called "centerfire." Most modern saddles, however, are full-rigged—that is the front (main) cinch is all the way forward and is supplemented by a rear cinch well back. This configuration reflects roping influence and isn't necessarily the best for the trail. Slim-built horses often suffer chafe in what might be called the "armpit" area of the front legs with full-rigged saddles. If you

A rebuilt, slick-forked 1885 saddle owned by Magnus Johnson, Emily Aadland's grandfather.

have a choice, specify a seven-eighths or three-quarter configuration with the front cinch back just a bit.

Once the saddle is on the horse's back over a pad or blanket, there's a correct order for attaching it to the animal. My constant reminder regards

Emily riding in a more modern deep-seat saddle.

the front cinch—"on first, off last." It's a refrain I won't let my clients forget. The reason is simple: the front cinch does most of the holding, though if a rear cinch is present it should be snugged tightly, not left hanging.

We fasten the front cinch first, then appendages such as rear cinch and breast collar, because we want the saddle to be secure before proceeding further. Attach the front cinch firmly, but not excessively tight. You can tighten it later before mounting. Now that it's in place, should a bee sting your horse you won't witness a rodeo that could end up with the saddle under the horse's belly, kicked to pieces, something that might happen if the spook occurred when only a breast collar or crupper had been attached.

When unsaddling, reverse the procedure. Get all appendages, breast collar, crupper, rear cinch loose, and remove anything tied to your saddle that adds heft or awkwardness when lifting it off. Only then release the front cinch and remove the saddle.

I usually wait until just before mounting to bridle my horse. Regardless of the type of bit (or bosal, if you fancy hackamore tradition), the accompanying photo of my friend Jerry shows a textbook illustration of bridling correctly. Starting at the shoulder and moving forward, Jerry controls the headstall with his right hand held above the horse's poll, lowering the bit, then raising it as the horse accepts it into his mouth. There's no coming at the horse from the front in his blind spot like an intimidating predator.

Proper bridling illustrated by the late Jerry Julson.

Always check the tightness of the front cinch before mounting. It should be very snug, but not choking tight. Mounting properly can allow a looser, more comfortable cinch. Sloppy mounting with your body weight well out to the side of the horse results in a hard push on the near stirrup when your weight hits it. Also, a narrower, high-withered horse can be mounted with the cinch at a more humane level of tension than a mutton-withered, round-barreled animal, assuming the saddle fits well. Mounting with a block (or a handy stump in the backcountry) can help as well.

Too often I see riders mount in a way that pulls the saddle harshly to the side. Mounting on the left (near) side of the horse, they grasp the horn with their left hand and the cantle of the saddle with the right, then pull to the side, and finally getting up. Unless you're young and fit, able to bounce into the saddle, this method tends to torque the saddle sideway to an excessive degree. It also puts you totally out of contact with the horse's mouth during the time you're mounting. Fixed in your left hand against the horn, the reins are immovable. Hopefully you've taken up some slack in the reins, perhaps holding the left with a bit more tension than the right, so that should your horse move off, he'll likely turn toward you. But however you've set them, they'll stay that way until you're in the saddle, and if the horse moves while you mount, you can do nothing about that.

There's a better way. Again take the slack out of the reins, keeping the left rein slightly tighter than the right. Grasp a handful of the horse's mane with your left hand about halfway up his neck. Grasp the saddle horn with your right hand or, if it gives you more leverage and you're tall enough, grip the far side of the pommel instead. Now your body is turned forward and your weight tends to stay closer to the animal. During the mounting process you can manipulate the reins with your left hand if necessary, checking the horse if he offers to move forward.

Mounting with left hand on neck holding mane, right on horn or cantle allows more control.

Of course, all of this is reversed if you mount on the right (off) side, and your horse should allow this. Mounting from both sides should be included in his elementary training. I'm not sure where our bias toward working on the left side of the horse originated, but I noticed in Iceland that both sides of the horse were used interchangeably, the riders hopping on one side or the other seemingly without preference. In the backcountry, where mounting blocks are absent and there's not always a handy stump to help you mount a tall horse, feeling confident to get on the right side is essential.

The trail often runs along a hillside, and mounting from the uphill side is an advantage.

HANDLING OBSTACLES

Before heading for the backcountry, you can simulate much (but not all) of what you'll encounter later by work in a corral or arena where you and the horse are comfortable. Among the simulated obstacles we use is a bright orange plastic irrigation tarp lying on the sand. It moves and makes a rustling sound when a horse steps on it. We also have a wooden trail bridge, poles that can be set up in several patterns, and various "scary" objects such as plastic bags hanging on the arena walls.

Whether you're training your horse from the beginning or testing the tolerance of a trained horse you're preparing for the backcountry, working with trail obstacles in the arena first will tell you much about what to expect later. It's completely normal for a horse to study, maybe even snort at, an object he's never encountered before. As I've said, the objective is not to dull his senses, but to help him cope with whatever signals they send.

I favor what I call a low-stress approach to trail obstacles. Out on the trail, the object can be nothing more intimidating than a bright-colored rock or trail sign, but the horse doesn't know it's harmless. The first step is to ride casually up to the obstacle and simply proceed if the horse acts confident to do so. But if he stops and snorts, walks sideways, or worse, shows serious resistance (attempting to rear, for instance) thus making it manifestly clear that he wants nothing to do with the object, then he needs some schooling.

If the resistance is mild, I may keep the horse just where he has stopped. If it's more serious, I may back off a little way until I feel him relax a bit. Through the process I try to keep him looking at the object, but one of the first things I do (if the terrain allows it) is to move him sideways a little way. That monocular vision horses have when viewing an object from the side may have caused the fright. Simply moving the horse slightly so he views it from a different angle may change the appearance and allow the horse to recognize the object as harmless.

Jennifer gives Scout a little time to check out the tarp, and then he walks across.

Again, Scout is given time to study, and when he's ready, moved forward and eventually across the trail bridge.

If that doesn't work I'll keep the horse looking at the offending item, petting him and reassuring him. Why not just ram my heels into him and force him past? Perhaps in an emergency (lightning cracking behind me and hail coming down) I might do that. But it's far better if he can learn for himself that the item is harmless. How about letting your partner's seasoned horse pass by, showing yours that it's safe to proceed? I've done that as well, but our first choice still should be letting the horse assimilate the object and become confident in its proximity.

Usually if your horse has some time to study you'll gradually feel him ease. Perhaps he'll take a deep breath. When that happens, move him forward, but only until he tenses again. Then repeat the procedure.

What if you try these things to no avail? Should you ever give up (assuming you don't really have to get past the obstacle), and admit defeat? I have the usual aversion to letting a horse get away with anything, to allowing him to win in a confrontation, and you certainly should avoid that. But sometimes safety comes first. If a horse is so frightened that he is attempting to rear, buck, or bolt, maybe it's best to handle this another day or in another way. Going up a steep sidehill I encountered a ditch my stallion refused to cross. He'd get to it, then give a couple of stiff hops downslope in a manner that was far from safe. Much as I hated to do it, I returned to the arena to do some groundwork and make a plan for overcoming the obstacle on another day. In this case, going out with a friend on a seasoned horse did the trick, and I hadn't "ruined" or "spoiled" my horse.

Should you get off to lead the animal past an obstacle he refuses steadfastly, in spite of your best efforts? Here again, some caveats apply. As in the above situation, put your safety first, and if you simply must pass the obstacle, but your horse is behaving dangerously, perhaps it's best to get off and lead. Do remember that for some reason horses see things differently with a rider aboard. Horses sometimes pass objects frequently, perhaps in their pastures, then find the same item strangely scary while carrying a rider. Leading a horse past an obstacle may soften his resistance to it. He'll hear the sound of his hooves on the plastic tarp you've laid out, and find in following you that the object isn't truly dangerous. But he may still resist after you mount up.

There comes a time when you've successfully worked your horse in the arena, when he's learned to cope with the obstacles you've set up, that it's time for the real thing. You can only do so much in the round pen and arena, only simulate to a certain degree. A few years ago CDs were marketed with all sorts of noises on them, which you could play loudly in the arena, allegedly to get your horse used to the sounds of trains, dogs, traffic, and so on. I was contacted by the creator of this particular idea. I pointed out that horses pick up on a whole array of sensual information, that simply hearing the recorded sounds was probably not enough to accustom the horse to the real thing. On-the-job training must come sooner or later.

But it's important to consider the horse's point of view when first getting him out on the trails and into the backcountry. Should you take a companion? Truthfully, the very best training is one-on-one, you and your horse. But going out alone isn't within the comfort zone of many riders, and that's understandable. However, going out with the wrong people and/or horses is the worst possible scenario.

My wife and I have bred naturally gaited Tennessee Walking Horses for nearly forty years. I tell clients who own gaited animals new to the backcountry to avoid most gaited horse organized trail rides, because too often the leaders of the rides, anxious to demonstrate their mounts' acumen, set a pace that is far too fast. Your poor animal, perhaps at the tail end of "snake dance," breaks gait to keep up. Yes, he may blow by obstacles in order to keep up with the other horses, but without time to study them, he learns little. Encountering the same obstacles later, you may find he acts as if he's never seen them. Worse, horses are herd animals and big groups tend to make your inexperienced horse forget his training in an effort to stay with the others at all costs.

If for safety you wish to go out with another rider, go out with just one, and choose the person and horse carefully. A horse with bad habits will tend to confuse your own animal and make things worse. A rider who doesn't understand what you wish to accomplish will prevent you and your horse from learning.

The ideal companion has a well-trained, steady, older horse. The rider is a patient person, willing to hang back as you teach your horse to pass an obstacle, willing to set a pace that suits you. With such a companion you can switch places, alternating between leading and following. If your companion's horse is calm, that demeanor may spread to your own mount. Unless you have an unusually complete obstacle array in your arena or corral, your horse may not have crossed water with a rider aboard until you take him out. Streams are a prime example of obstacles that stimulate the horse with a whole complement of smell and touch sensations. Further, a horse's vision is limited by them—muddy streams don't allow the horse to predict what lies under the water, and horses have a healthy skepticism about bogs and swamps.

That skepticism can be a good thing. I once forced a tall black gelding named Marauder (a name which was a bit of a joke because it didn't match his disposition) over what I was certain was dry ground between two pine trees. I couldn't understand the horse's reluctance and near-refusal to go there, but that soon changed. What Marauder could detect with his superior senses—that there was a spring under that innocent-looking ground—I could not. We sank through the dry crust beyond knee level, but Marauder gave several healthy lunges and pulled us through. We were alone in the mountains, not a healthy situation in which to bog down a horse.

Emily gives Scooter a bit of time, but keeps him looking at the water.

On our ranch, horses are reared on flood-irrigated pastures, so the feeling of chilly water around the pasterns and cannon bones is normal for them. But that's not true for all horses. Daisy, a grade pinto, came to our ranch from dryland country where water was scarce and all drinking was from stock tanks. She had never waded in water, and her first experience created quite a sensation. But I suspect there are many stall and paddock-raised horses with similar backgrounds.

Horses will often cross a wide stream readily, but balk at small ones and even at mud puddles. This has much to do with vision. It's as though they can view a larger stream, take stock of it, then proceed. A tiny stream may fall closer to their blind spot as they view it, and they perhaps think it may indicate a crevice of some sort.

For the horse that's totally new to water crossings, the help of that companion with her steady, well-trained horse is probably a good idea. For most horses, though, streams should be approached like any other obstacle, and the techniques are the same. First, do make sure you're crossing in a safe spot, preferably an existing ford that's been used by horses. A cattle crossing (evidenced both by cattle droppings and the tracks of cloven hooves) may not be safe for your horse. Bovines handle boggy areas with more skill and less excitement than horses. Water crossings in the backcountry can be tricky, too, for another reason. Rainstorms and snow melt can raise a stream during the day. The stream that can be crossed in the morning on your way up the mountain may change drastically during the day and represent an unsafe obstacle when you return later that afternoon.

In my experience, a good share of the time even an inexperienced horse walks into the water readily. But if he doesn't, give him a bit of time. Keep him looking at the spot on the other side you intend to land after crossing. If necessary move him to one side or the other so he gets a different perspective. If he resists, back off until he relaxes, then "take up the slack" by moving him toward the stream.

Once in the water, keep your eye on that spot on the other side where you intend to exit the stream, and keep your horse looking there as well. Avoid looking down at swift water—you may find it makes you dizzy, and it unbalances the horse as well. For your horse to go straight, you must be straight, a principle that applies to riding generally.

Crossing a larger stream on Redstar, Emily looks straight ahead at the point she'll emerge on the far bank.

GOOD SPOOKS, BAD SPOOKS, AND FAKE SPOOKS

All horses spook, and I look with great skepticism on claims that any horse is "bombproof," "foolproof," or otherwise infallible. No human is infallible. How can a horse be expected to withstand anything his world dishes out without ever making a mistake?

As we've said, a great deal of horse training involves teaching our horses to resist their innate instinct to flee at the sudden appearance of something new and potentially dangerous. Watch a herd of horses, and you'll eventually see one spook with the others following. After a while, when they've run a ways, they'll turn around and look back, trying to figure out just what had scared them. Their motto seems to be, "Run first, question later."

I suspect most backcountry rider injuries (and those in more domestic surroundings as well) are due to spooks. The horse encounters a deer or a dog or a bicycle suddenly, jumps sideways, and the rider falls off and is injured. The best riders don't unseat so easily, but it's a sad fact that many riders today ride too little to keep their skills honed. Too many as well are heavy in the torso and weak in the legs, and some sit on horses as passengers, not really riding, not really putting enough pressure on their stirrups to maintain a secure seat. (More on these things later.) And, of course, people simply get careless.

So how can I classify any spook as a "good spook?" The good spook reminds us that our horse is well-trained. Usually it's just a start, a small jerk in place. I don't believe you can apply Freudian psychology to horses, but if you could it might go something like this. Remember your Psychology 101 class? The Id referred to animal instinct, the Ego referred to unthinking control of that Id, and the Superego referred to intellectual (rational) control, the sort gained by education.

Training, whether of horses or people, involves education (Superego), but what we're ultimately seeking is that unthinking reaction gained by training, the Ego. Perfect examples among humans are soldiers, policemen, EMT responders, nurses, and others in professions where there's often no time to think. These people must react, but react correctly, and that's something that is gained only by training. That's why all such professions emphasize rehearsal, practice, and drills. And for the most part, we train horses the same way.

So good spooks are the sort exhibited when a horse responds to a surprise by no more than a jerk or snort. The horse's animal instinct to bolt is brought immediately under control by something like the Ego. Unthinkingly, your horse checks his impulse to flee, because he's been thoroughly trained to do so. His checked response reminds us that he hasn't been desensitized—all senses are well intact—but he has been trained. I respond to good spooks with a reassuring word and a pat on the neck.

Bad spooks vary in intensity, but all are undesirable and potentially dangerous. Even well-trained horses suffer bad spooks occasionally, but if the training has been thorough, those can usually be defused. The horse may attempt to bolt, but a good rider can normally bring the animal under control.

However, there's the occasional horse that simply loses it. I crossed a river once, followed by a woman on a mature and supposedly well-trained Quarter Horse she'd recently purchased. We crossed the stream on a rocky, shallow bar, flanked both up and downstream by deeper pools. My horse scrambled up the bank, and the client followed. When we stopped for an instant her horse shook like a dog, hesitated a second, then launched into the most frightening and most violent bucking session I've ever witnessed.

There was no rhyme or reason to it. After three or four hard bucks, heading upstream on the edge of a vertical bank, the horse bucked right off the edge, about eight feet or so above the water, the rider flying off and landing on the water what with what we'd have called as kids a "belly flop." Concerned with the welfare of the woman, I lost sight of the horse as he continued to attempt to buck in the water. The rider, it turned out, was one of the toughest I've known. She floated with the current over toward the bank where I'd dismounted, and I reached down, grabbed her arm, and hauled her ashore.

She was unhurt, a bit shaken, but wanted mostly a warm shower to warm up. We were thankful that the water had been relatively deep where she landed; had she been bucked off in the shallow riffle, serious injury would have been inevitable. I sent her back across the stream on my own horse, which in turn was ponied back to me by another rider. The woman walked the short distance back to the arena and was completely recovered by the time I got there. We laughed about the two wide-eyed fly fishermen who had witnessed the entire event.

Thankfully, most bad spooks are not this bad. I'd witnessed a horse that totally lost it, without seeming provocation beyond a crossing of chilly water. Had that riverbank been a hundred-foot cliff, the horse would have bucked his way off it just as readily, for his reaction was irrational, unseeing, unfeeling, and terribly dangerous. Most bad spooks indicate some additional training is in order, but in my book, this one was terminal. Had the horse been mine, I'd never have mounted him again, and his owner had the same good judgment, finishing the clinic on a borrowed horse.

Yes, some clinicians will tell you that there are no bad horses, only bad trainers. They repeat other such gushing platitudes that elevate the horse above the human, make him into a sort of Noble Creature of Nature that is only bad because an experience made him so. Sorry, but I don't buy it. There are psychotic horses just as there are psychotic humans, and I'd just witnessed the incredible violence that one such could dish out.

Again, most bad spooks do not fall into this category. Even during a spook, most horses look out for their own welfare and don't go into an irrational state. Most simply try to get away from whatever scares them, and the spook overcomes their training. An action we call the one-rein stop is the key element in bringing the horse under control.

Based on the premise that brought into a tight circle, pulled around tightly with its head neither far down nor elevated above normal carriage, a

Before the one-rein stop, horses must be trained from the first ride to yield to the snaffle bit. Trainer Jennifer Franco teaching a soft yield on the very first ride.

horse can neither buck nor run away. It's not quite that conclusive—a horse can still make things pretty uncomfortable for the rider in that bent position, but it's certainly more difficult for him to either run or buck.

But several things are necessary for the one-rein stop to work. First, the rider has to be cool enough to remember to apply it. Many riders tend to seize up when trouble occurs, their reaction being to pull back hard on both reins. That may stop the horse, but it also may make him what we call "light in front," tending toward rearing, one of the most dangerous actions a horse can make. Rearing can lead to going over backward, an action that can be fatal to the rider.

Further, the rider applying the one-rein stop must remember to give slack with the off-side rein. If you're pulling the horse around to the left, the right side must have slack. That can be difficult to remember in a tense situation. And the horse, too, must be used to yielding to the pull from that one rein.

The way to accomplish this, of course, is practice. The one-rein stop should be rehearsed in the arena and practiced frequently. Sit on your horse in a resting position and practice drawing up one rein and bringing his head around. This is an essential element of foundation training, but it's possible your horse was not trained with this step, so practice it. Should your horse act up in any way during your early experience with him, apply the one-rein stop.

Fake spooks are a learned response. Somewhere along the way a horse has learned that if he feigns fear, he'll get out of an unpleasant task. Horses with weak or indecisive owners are most likely to develop fake spooks. Dog trainers are often asked to straighten out a pet that learns his humans will react in a certain way if he growls. Instead of straightening him out early in the game, such dog owners create monsters, big bully dogs that growl if they don't get their way.

Horses can learn that a fear reaction can get them what they want, usually out of a task such as passing a particular object that scared them early in the game. Perhaps the first time in the tractor's proximity they were actually frightened, and a show of resistance caused the rider to turn around and go home. Now in that very same spot in the lane, the tractor long gone from the scene, the horse acts up in some way, slows down or jigs or walks sideways, and the frightened owner does the same thing—turns back toward

Constantly practice the one-rein stop.

home. The fake spook gets the horse out of work and he milks it for all he can.

Put an assertive rider on that horse, give him a quirt or a riding crop, and watch what happens. At the horse's favorite place in the lane his antics bring him a sharp whack on the rear, and suddenly the horse is no longer frightened at that spot. But unless the original rider toughens up, the horse will try again.

The trick with fake spooks is detecting them. Is the horse truly frightened, or is he trying to evade? Recall the animal's history at this particular spot on the trail or when encountering a similar object. If the spook is fake, assertive riding will normally nip it in the bud. As a side note, observe that scary objects on the trail are suddenly benign on the way home, when the horse is anxious to return to his buddies.

The barn-soured horse is probably the epitome of the fake-spook problem. Rarely is a horse with this particular problem truly afraid to be out alone. He just has a vast preference for being with his friends, and he also has probably not accepted his rider as his leader, as the second half of his "herd of two." The barn-soured horse will go a certain distance from his home paddock and friends, and then begin to act restive. Take him farther and he'll begin to whinny, then, if he's truly spoiled, jig or buck or simply refuse to go farther. Sometimes his antics are annoying, sometimes truly dangerous, and in any case, he's convinced his past riders to give up and let him return. And each time this happens, each time he gets what he wants, the bad habit becomes more tightly ingrained.

As with so many things, prevention is the best cure. Horses should be ridden out alone as soon as they're well-trained enough to be relatively safe. But too many professional trainers take horses for either thirty, sixty, or ninety days, with most training happening in the round pen or arena or on a very limited acreage around their facility. Not everyone, even professionals, is comfortable with long solo rides, and not everyone has terrain nearby that's suitable.

On our ranch I have options not available to some. Here, horses are often run in several small groups in this pasture or that. The horse in training that gets too attached to his buddies can be moved from pasture to pasture so that he doesn't form deep dependence on any one horse—that seems to help. I've also completely isolated a horse on which I'm focused, put him in his own corral, made him dependent on me for his "herd," his food, water, and attention.

On a young horse going out, I often give a sharp heel cue or say "quit!" even when the animal merely whinnies for the friends he's leaving behind. Should he hesitate or act up because of the departure, a one-rein stop in place is in order—that is bringing the horse around tightly for several revolutions, then turning him the other way. But truthfully, we've had few problems in this area, again because our horses are ridden out alone from the start.

When you purchase a trained horse, however, the situation is entirely different. The seller or the trainer demonstrates the horse in a corral or arena and all seems fine. But at home you find the horse steadfastly refuses

On the first ride out I normally accompany the trainer, but there's no substitute for riding out alone to prevent the barn-soured horse. After this ride, Jennifer will take the mare on many solo rides.

to go out by himself. Before you buy, insist on seeing the horse ridden out from the barn, preferably for a considerable distance. Some buyers offer trial periods during which you can check for barn-soured tendencies. If you ride with another person, put the new horse in front at least part of the time. Barn-soured horses are often followers.

BASIC BACKCOUNTRY RIDING

So you're on the trail, relaxed and enjoying the ride, but hopefully watchful and aware as well. No matter how seasoned your horse, never let your senses sleep, and don't let your horse forget that he's at work. As long as you're on him, his time sheet has been punched, he's on the job, and he should be engaged. A cowboy told me his father impressed upon him that you should never let your horse go to sleep, because you have no idea what he'll do when he suddenly wakes up! Sleep, here, didn't mean a human sort of slumber, but simply a forgetting of purpose, of the fact that the horse was at work.

Today there is much emphasis on riding with a loose rein, but I prefer the term "light rein." Loose rein implies what old-timers call a "belly in the reins," that is a downward loop of slack line. Riding with reins in that fashion disengages your rein hand from the horse. (Note that "hand" here is singular—all good backcountry horses neck rein, but that's the subject of the next chapter.) While some well-trained horses proceed down the trail just fine with loose reins, what happens when you meet a bear on the trail? Virtually all horses are capable of a "bad spook" under certain circumstances, and your defense for that, the one-rein-stop, is momentarily unavailable if you have to reel in rein to make contact with the horse's mouth to pull him around. In the time it takes to pull in the slack, bad things can happen.

Light rein to me means an amount of slack that is just taken up when the horse moves his neck forward in the natural telescoping fashion that accompanies the walk. In other words, light contact is just barely made at that point with just a bit of slack when the head telescopes back. The horse knows you are there in contact with him, but the reins give him room to walk freely with natural head carriage. And you, the rider, have the ability to quickly check the horse if needed.

Rough country riding entails some techniques that may seem counter-intuitive. For instance, when riding on a ledge trail cut into the side of a hill (or cliff), if you have to turn around and head the other way (that bear a hundred yards up the trail doesn't seem interested in moving) it's important to turn your horse toward the drop-off side of the trail. This may scare you, but it's the safest way. The reason is that for all their acumen, horses don't always know exactly where their hind legs lie in relation to ground that may not be safe. If you turn them toward the drop-off, they know how much room they have to work with. Like you, the horse has a strong sense of self-preservation.

Many years ago I took my two young sons on their very first pack trip. Straining to get a photograph, I turned my horse back toward them on a rocky trail lined on both sides with boulders and thick shrubbery. Without warning, my big, long-backed gelding fell down flat, rolling partway over onto my leg. Thankfully, the fall was gentle enough that neither he nor I was seriously hurt. The cause was a hole on the side of the trail that I hadn't seen, but had I been aware of it and turned toward it, I suspect Rockytop would have sniffed it out. Don't count on a horse knowing exactly where his hind legs are stepping.

Assuming you're off trail, short steep banks, such as those on a big ditch or railroad right of way, are often safest when negotiated straight up or straight down, not slanting sideways. Should a horse's legs slip out from under him on a slick sidehill, he'll likely fall on your uphill leg. But if the bank is a not a tall one, and you're heading straight down, the horse, if he loses footing, will usually brace his legs and slide straight to the bottom. Going up, unless the footing is truly treacherous, he can usually scramble straight up.

I've only had one sidehill mishap, but it resulted in some pain. My son and I were trying to retrieve a lost calf that had strayed into a neighbor's land and become separated from its mother. A calf in such a situation is irrational and flighty, likely to run in any direction except the one you wish. It seemed most effective for son Steve to work on foot while I brought my good gelding Little Mack for the task.

We got the calf headed toward our neighbor's corrals, and all seemed well. I had Little Mack in a nice canter along the contour of a side hill, not the best footing perhaps, but decent enough that I felt safe—that is until we suddenly hit a green wet area where an irrigation ditch had leaked into the field below. Little Mack's legs went out from under him downhill as if on grease, his body falling uphill. The ground was soft enough that my leg withstood the impact, but my torso must have taken a bit of a shock. Although I didn't verify broken ribs with X-rays, the fact that I couldn't sneeze or laugh without severe pain for several weeks suggested ribs were broken or severely bruised.

Body position when going steeply uphill and downhill is often incorrectly taught. I've known many clients who have been told to lean forward when going uphill, back when going downhill. That's half right. Yes, when progressing steeply uphill you should lean forward. That helps the horse by keeping your weight closer to his center of gravity. Just don't lean so far forward that should the horse suddenly raise his head, his neck encounters your nose. That can happen! And, as with downhill riding, give the horse some extra rein. He needs freedom to pump his shoulders and neck, to get his hind feet up under him, and you don't want to hamper that by keeping him on a tight rein.

This descent is far steeper than it appears in the photograph, but Emily avoids leaning back, which can prevent the horse from getting his hind legs up under him.

Going down requires the same freedom and the same need to keep your weight toward the horse's center of gravity. *The Man from Snowy River* notwithstanding, the US Army Cavalry taught riders to lean forward, not back, when going downhill, particularly at high speed. Old training films show riding that most would find frightening today, but you'll note that leaning back on fast descents was avoided. Why? Leaning backward makes it difficult for the horse to get his hind legs up under him, and if he can't do that on a steep descent, he may fall.

Luckily, most backcountry riders today don't have to worry about battlefield scenarios, about stressing their horses through obstacles at high speed. But we should keep in mind that the horse's center of gravity is fairly far forward. On most horses it's located a short distance behind his front elbows and about a third of the way up his body. We'll discuss how this affects the horse's weight-carrying ability later in this book. But it's important to remember that leaning backward on descents can hamper the horse.

No, it's probably not necessary at the speeds we use in the backcountry to lean forward while going downhill, but try to stay perpendicular or nearly so. One rider expressed it this way: "Going downhill I like to be able to look straight down at the saddle horn." In other words, he meant keeping his body at approximately the same angle in relation to the horse as he would have been doing on level ground. That posture, along with plenty of free rein, will normally allow the horse to proceed down a steep slope safely.

OPEN COUNTRY AND CRITTERS ON THE TRAIL

Although we often characterize backcountry horses as "trail" horses, it's worth noting that much riding, particularly in the West, involves few trails, unless they're the numerous cow paths that crisscross western rangeland. Cows, incidentally, are pretty good engineers when it comes to establishing trails that angle up and down hills at acceptable grades. Unfortunately, they lay out their trails where they can walk, not where your tall horse can go with a tall rider. Too often in making use of a cow (or wild game) trail, you run into overhanging bushes which make staying in the saddle impossible.

The Big Open can cause its own challenges for horses. Horses are open-country animals, a bit farsighted, and happiest when they can see what's stirring off in the distance. On a trail through heavy timber, your horse tends to rely on you and on any other horses that happen to be along

Riding in the Big Open off trail is an entirely different experience for the horse than riding on a tree-lined trail.

on the trail. Even a relatively green colt can often be ridden on such a trail, sandwiched between a horse in front and a horse behind.

Open country is a different story. Here the horse is likely to be more self-reliant. A herd of horses far in the distance won't escape his notice, and if you need to ride through such a herd, hang on—this can turn into a challenge, a direct war between your horse's natural instincts to run with a herd versus the discipline he's learned in training. On a young, green horse I avoid such a scenario as best I can.

It's not common today for ranchers to run herds of horses on the range with a stallion present, but that was not always so. If you ride where "wild" horses (properly, "feral" or the offspring of feral horses) occupy the range, should you encounter a herd with a stallion, you might follow the advice of a Norwegian American rancher, who was my boss when I was just fourteen years old and working my first summer ranch job. If his reaction to the herd of horses we encountered sounds harsh, I can only say it was offered in self-defense.

The horses we encountered were the rancher's own, not feral. Like many ranchers a half century ago, he ran a stallion out on the range with his broodmare herd. It was customary then (perhaps required by law) to post signs on access points to the range stating "stallion at large." But there's another clue always present when you enter a stallion's territory: there will be mounds of manure at access points, the stallion's warning that he rules this particular area.

Saddling up, I was thrilled with the break from the drudgery of feeding hogs and keeping the dairy barn clean. Riding the range with the boss was a treat for a town-raised kid. When the group of a dozen or more mares showed up, accompanied by a prancing palomino stallion that tossed his mane and whinnied, I was initially impressed—until I felt the gelding I was riding come alive in ways I wasn't sure I could handle.

The rancher shouted at the stallion and yelled to me in his accent, "Get off—trow rocks!" That's what we did—dismounted, pitching rocks in the general direction of the stallion while the rancher yelled certain phrases not altogether familiar to a preacher's kid. The stallion cavorted, then gathered his mares and galloped off. Before we remounted, the rancher took time to explain to me that you never let a range stallion get too close to you. The stallion sees your horse as an imposter, a challenger, and you don't want to be mounted when the stallion attacks. Most stallions, though, have enough experience with humans to respond when they're being chased off, and that was the case with the rancher's palomino.

Riding in the Big Open is wonderful in its way, however, and more backcountry horsemen should utilize the West's vast regions of open sage country, often public and open to riders. Much of it is BLM (Bureau of Land Management) land, and riding in it puts you in common with much of the

West's horseback history. And, as a benefit, going off trail is one of the very best ways to perfect your horse's neck rein (the subject of the next chapter).

A trail ride in open country.

Other kinds of livestock can also pose hazards, mostly because of potential spooks rather than any hostility. With cows the main issue is your horse's past experience. His first trip through them may be dicey, but riding with a calm horse, one used to cows, will tend to defuse that. I've known backcountry riders who've arranged with ranchers or farmers to pasture their horses with cows, just to get them used to the animals, their appearance, smell, and sounds.

Most range cows are used to being worked by people on horseback and few, even the bulls, are likely to be hostile. A good wave and shout if they get too close will usually start them moving away. The same is true of sheep, though in my experience, horses are more likely to be afraid of them than of cows. I don't live in an area that contains feral hogs, so I suspect my horses would find them threatening.

Introducing a young mare to cows.

Among wildlife, all but the very most urban horses probably are familiar with deer. Wildlife biologists estimate there may be more deer in the US than when Europeans first arrived on the continent. It's the sudden, quick appearance of deer that is likely to cause a spook. But moose are a different story. Perhaps it's their sheer size, but horses tend to be extremely frightened of moose. One of our best geldings remembers too well an encounter with bull moose in a particular drainage. He still snorts at the spot where we encountered the bull, and he attempts to get out of the valley as quickly as he can.

You can't train your horse for all wild and domestic animal encounters that may occur. In the case of domestic animals, give your horse as much exposure as possible. But meeting a grizzly bear on the trail, if it ever happens, is likely to be an once-in-a-lifetime event, and it's not one for which you can prepare by actual exposure. This is why we must train for "good spooks," for the control that comes to a horse when his training outweighs his natural inclination to run. Key to this is the one-rein-stop. Practice it, and use it even when minor spooks occur. Make it second nature, replacing any natural tendency you have to panic and simply pull back on both reins.

You can't train in advance for everything you might meet on the trail! The one-rein stop is the answer.

SPEED CONTROL

Fundamental to all horse training is the idea of impulsion. The first steps in training a colt normally involve asking him to move forward and if necessary, enforcing that request with a cue from a longe whip or the long lead rope favored by many today.

But horses aren't all the same. Some lean toward lazy, some the polar opposite. As I write this I've just returned from a three-day elk hunt in the mountains on which I rode a four-year-old gray gelding I've named Chief. Chief is extremely gentle, comes across the pasture to be caught, and exudes kindness. He reminds me of a big dog in this respect. He wants to hang out with me, and when released in a pasture after a long ride he stays alongside me until I leave, rather than galloping off to rejoin his mates.

But Chief has a turbocharged V-8 motor. He's been trained with a soft touch, so there's never a problem holding him back—he operates on a light rein with just slight rein contact—but release that ounce of pressure and he picks up speed. This suits me. He's the type of horse I've aimed for in my breeding program for nearly forty years, and the fact that Chief covers

Lancelot, like Chief, had such a big motor and yearn to go that he could have become a "charger," but Jennifer trained him to go at the speed desired and to stand and visit with a slack rein.

ground in a smooth flat-walk and running walk is pure gravy. On the trip mentioned above, though not properly conditioned and still not mature, Chief showed no signs of being the slightest bit tired until, perhaps, the third day, even though the hunt meant rough-terrain riding of many miles each day carrying a heavy man and his gear.

But poorly trained, Chief could have become what some people call "chargey." That sort of horse and his polar opposite, the type I call a laggard, present problems on the trail, and neither is desirable. Fortunately, good training can help either fall into the right groove, which is simply this: a horse should proceed down the trail at the speed you select, neither slowing nor speeding up until asked, and he should do this without your heels in his flanks nor a heavy restraining hand on the reins. The end result should be similar to cruise control in a car.

In my youth I worked for various ranches, and as junior member of the workforce, I never was given the most desirable horse. The type I learned to detest was the lazy horse that required a kick nearly every step to get his work done. Top that with a nasty disposition and you had the complete package, the horse that resented work but was quick to crow-hop if you required him to do it. Old-timers normally handled this sort of horse with a heavy quirt applied to the behind, and, if the horse wanted to buck because of that, a run straight up a hill.

Usually, this sort of horse isn't lacking in physical ability. His laziness may be partly that, but more likely, it's a learned response to a nagging rider who never demands performance. Perhaps his impulsion training wasn't thorough before riding. Perhaps he's been allowed to snatch grass or to take unscheduled rests his rider hasn't ordered. He may have convinced a weak rider that he was tired.

The laggard has probably been given continual cues, most likely kicks with the heels and verbal commands to move out. And he's come to demand such cues at virtually every step. The solution may not appeal to you, may not be acceptable to you, but it normally works: instead of digging your heels into such a horse, give him a very hard whack on the rear with a quirt, crop, or if you have neither, a switch you can pick up on the trail. When you whack, be prepared for a jump—but at least it will be forward. The horse is likely to speed up, what you want, and as long as he's going at a decent walk, get off his butt—literally. But when he slows, whack again.

Don't nag. Constant cues not taken seriously remind me of nagging parents, who seem to continually yell at their kids but with no result. The hard cue you give the lagging horse is less abusive, I believe, than the constant nagging of heels in the rib cage. And, since impulsion comes from behind, a spank on the rear is more effective than kicking, even if spurs are involved. But the key is the old principle of pressure/release. The whack is pressure— the release comes by his doing the right thing, speeding up and quitting unscheduled stops.

In many respects the "chargey" horse has the same issues, only with a different personality. He, too, has been made what he is by lax training and perhaps by too much exposure to fast trail rides led by riders who push the envelope. Gaited horses, with their natural "go," are susceptible to becoming chargey, but it can happen to any horse with a big motor.

Here again, prevention is easier than cure. Softness on the bit, built in the round pen with much stopping in place, insisting on the horse remaining in place with loose rein, constant turning right and left (giving to the bit) with pressure release all can help.

But too often the scenario is something like this: beyond the round pen the horse wants to go, especially when he's turned around toward home. The rider keeps up a steady bit pressure with no release, which the horse resists by returning the pressure. Once back at the arena the rider exclaims that the bit he's using is inadequate. And thus begins a succession of attempts to find a bit that holds the horse back, all the time with the same approach to riding—pressure on the horse that is never released until the chargey horse becomes unpleasant or even unsafe to ride.

Just as a hard kick or slap on the butt, followed by a release at the proper response, helps the lagging horse, a sharp jerk on the reins, then release when the horse slows down, is better medicine for the charging horse. Again, don't nag. Steady pressure without release is nagging. A sharp jerk will not ruin or hurt your horse. He'll slow down and you can reward him by instant release of pressure.

It's wonderful we live in an era when much attention is paid to the well-being of the horse, avoiding inflicting pain or hurting him in any way. That said, there are many horses that have become unmanageable, because their riders were terribly worried they'd somehow hurt their animals. When a gentle ninety-pound woman told me she was afraid of hurting her 1,100-pound horse if she gave him an assertive cue, I told her about Razzy.

Razzy was the family miniature horse that pulled a cart and took our grandchildren on rides, well-supervised ones because he had a mind of his own. The little gelding was running free with a mixed herd of mares, geldings, and retired horses on our east range the day we discovered one of our mares had foaled a bit early, before we'd returned her to the ranch headquarters. She was off by herself with the foal, and the rest of the herd hadn't discovered her and the newborn, a good thing.

I drove the pickup over to the mare, hoping to avoid notice, but to no avail. The herd came on a run. I dropped the tailgate of the pickup, snatched up the foal, and laid her in the bed of the pickup, holding her down with one hand as best I could. Emily would catch the mare, and we'd drive through the gate and out of the pasture, then reunite mare and foal safely away from a herd of horses that wouldn't intentionally hurt the foal, but likely would, out of curiosity, separate it from its dam.

But something got into Razzy. Perhaps he was thrilled to see a little horse. I only know he let out high-pitched squeals and charged toward us. He literally tried to climb into the back of the pickup, all the time letting loose with ear-piecing squeals, while I tried to hold the foal in place with my left hand while fending off Razzy with my right. I thumped him on the forehead with my fist in attempt to keep him back. No effect. I thumped him harder. He didn't even seem to feel it. Finally I whacked him hard, really hard, and my hand went limp with pain. I'd broken it. In an attempt to keep Razzy back I'd hit him so hard I broke my hand and the effect on the little horse was virtually nonexistent. I did manage to get the tailgate up, then climb into the back of the pickup to hold the foal with my one good arm, and we eventually straightened out the mess, Razzy squealing the whole while.

So I taught the very first session of the clinic on which this book is based with a broken hand. And I tell folks like that timid woman that the idea they'll hurt a horse by a corrective cue with the reins or a motivating quirt on his behind is ludicrous. To hurt her horse the woman would have to turn into a sadistic monster, use some sort of a weapon, and do unspeakable things. She could, however, hurt the horse, and probably shorten its useful life, by allowing it to become the monster, by refusing to correct it when necessary, because of timidity. Yes, she wants her horse to be her partner, but it *must* be the junior partner, must respect her as leader, and accept her discipline when such is necessary.

The chargey horse can be handled in other ways as well. If he wants to proceed too fast, remember the in-place version of the one rein stop. Turn the horse round and round in place, then proceed. If he wants to go too fast, then do it again. This, too, is pressure/release. No horse really likes being pulled into a tight circle. That's pressure. Allowing him to proceed down the trail with a light rein is release. Even a hardheaded horse will usually figure out it's probably better to accommodate you, the rider, by going down the trail at the speed you desire.

And what is that speed? It's the one you choose, but most likely in the backcountry, it'll be some version of the walk. Faster gaits are only safe on certain trails and certain circumstances. But we're talking a snappy, ambitious walk, not a pokey one. We'll touch on improving the walk (and other gaits) in the next chapter.

CHAPTER FIVE

THE NECK REIN
AND THE SIDE PASS

If I were asked just what marks both the backcountry horse and the western horse, what single attribute evokes it, it would not be a type of saddle, a certain breed, a color, or a rider dressed a particular way. Envision riders working their way down a mountain trail leading pack mules and you'll always notice one particular thing: the horses are ridden with one hand only, the other hand free to grasp a mule's lead rope, to fend off branches growing close to the trail, or if ridden by a cowboy, to swing a lariat rope.

The neck rein has long been an essential ingredient of working saddle horses in other capacities as well. Cavalrymen had to be able to swing a saber with one hand, their horses well trained enough to withstand the extreme stress of battle yet kept fully under control by a single hand on the reins. Cowboys could not have performed their various tasks without a free hand, and indeed, early cowboy trainers refused to put a second hand on the reins even when starting a colt (not necessarily a good thing, but one ingrained in their culture).

I'm old enough to remember when western-oriented horse magazines rarely published a photo of anyone riding a horse with a rein in each hand. Yet, today in such publications one often sees riders "plow reining," as the old timers would have called it. In the case of a colt being started, okay—but a mature horse that requires both hands on the reins is not a backcountry horse.

Nor is it a western horse. I can think of two schools of horsemanship being widely promoted on social media, one with the word "Cowboy" in front of it, the other with the word "Western." Look at the Facebook pages for each and you see some nice horses doing some nice things—but it's all done with a hand on each rein, and there's nothing cowboy or western about that, unless the rider is on a newly started colt.

So what changed? The answer may lie in fixation with the round pen, reluctance to leave it, and people's misinterpretation of what they see being done there. The videos made by many trainers show colts being started with emphasis on softness and responsiveness in the early stages of bit training. Direct reining with the snaffle bit has become the norm for these early lessons. But fewer videos exist of the stages of training that should follow.

Another reason may be schools of horsemanship that feature levels of training for both horse and rider and which place the neck rein in an advanced stage to which most clients never aspire. This contrasts with old-time western training in which the neck rein was taught from the very first ride.

Still another reason for the decline of the neck rein may be the decline of the need for the working horse. More horses today are ridden for simple pleasure. Although having to handle one's horse with a rein in each hand does not suit my own idea of pleasure, many feel otherwise, and many disciplines (jumping and dressage, for instance) involve horses ridden with a specialized rein.

But spend a day in the mountains on a horse with a finished neck rein, two slim and supple leather reins in your hand, cueing the horse in the direction desired by the slightest movement of that hand, and you'll quickly understand why working horsemen across the globe train their horses to perform in this fashion. For a left turn, you merely shift your hand a couple of inches to the left of the saddle horn. You're scarcely aware you're guiding the horse.

The good news is that it's very easy to train a horse to neck rein, starting with the first few rides on a colt. And, most mature horses whose training has lacked the neck rein take to it easily. We're considering, of course, neck reining, not *reining* in the competitive sense. Reining as a sport and arena show activity has a totally different set of requirements and objectives. For the backcountry we don't want or need a horse that will spin at the slightest touch of rein. And we're certainly not going to care about a sliding stop done on specialized slick-bottom shoes.

Before we get started a word about bits. Walk into a large tack store and look at their bit display. It's likely to be overwhelming. How on earth does one know what will work best? Only an extremely knowledgeable horseman can likely name all the individual types and varieties available or explain the intended use of each.

Bits of one sort or another have been used for a very long time. In the classic *The Art of Horsemanship*, written around 450 BCE, Greek general Xenophon discusses bits frequently, and cautions the reader not to be heavy-handed with them. And in the Old Testament, Psalm 32, King David writes, "Do not be like a horse or a mule, without understanding/ whose temper must be curbed with bit and bridle,/else it will not stay near you."

So over several thousand years bits have branched out into all sorts of varieties intended for particular purposes. But we can simplify. All bits really fall into one of two categories. Either they're nonleverage or leverage. If they have no leverage, that simply means three ounces of pressure tugged on one rein will result in three ounces of pressure to the side of the horse's mouth. Leverage bits, on the other hand, increase the amount of pressure applied by the use of shanks (levers) and the fulcrum formed by the curb

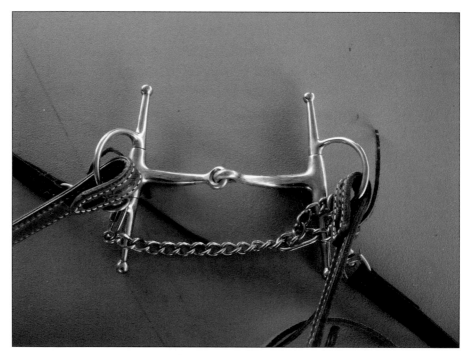

Snaffle bit, this one of the "full cheek variety," with bars to distribute the pull along the horse's mouth.

strap under the horse's jaw. They do this in varying amount, depending on several factors.

Nonleverage bits are called snaffles. They have no shanks. The reins attach to a ring at the corner of the mouth. Add shanks to a snaffle (as in what's commonly called a Tom Thumb bit) and it's no longer a snaffle, even though some tack catalogs call it such.

There is much confusion about snaffle bits. Unfortunately some misinformation is spread by clinicians who have frightened clients into thinking the snaffle is the only humane bit and the only bit with which their uneducated hands can trusted lest they do something horribly inhumane to the horse.

First, let's remember that it's not training devices for the most part (bits, crops, longe whips, long lead ropes, spurs, etc.) that are inherently severe—it's how these devices are used. (There *are* cruel training devices, certainly—we'll confine them to the ranks of the illegal and immoral.) Certainly some devices have more leverage or more potential to inflict pain than others, but that merely means they must be used with more care, lighter hands and gentler feet. A light touch with spurs is likely to be kinder than a hard kick with bare heels.

Secondly there's nothing inherently gentle about the snaffle bit. While it has no leverage, it does have the ability to pinch the mouth when used improperly. And proper use of the snaffle is as a direct rein bit, one rein at a time, with the other rein giving slack. If you pull straight back on both reins the snaffle pinches. It should be used from the saddle the same way it's used when driving horses in harness. That second requirement, giving the horse free rein on one side to make up for the tightened rein on the other, is one of the things most difficult to teach beginning horsemen.

Curbs vary tremendously in leverage and the variety is vast, but here are a couple of guidelines. Long shanks tend to provide more leverage than shorter ones, but with this caveat: the ratio between portion of the shank in front of the bit and the portion behind it also determine leverage. If the front portion is twice as long as the rear, that's a two-to-one ratio. Thus shank length alone doesn't determine leverage, and there are other factors as well, such as adjustment of the curb strap. We'll touch on these issues later.

We start our colts with a snaffle bit, and I prefer the type often called a full-cheek snaffle. Basically, that means the snaffle rings have an additional

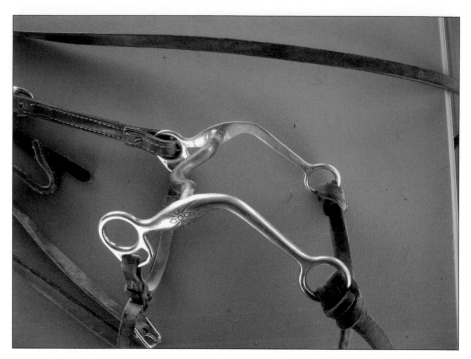

Mild curb bit of the "grazing" variety, with swept-back shanks to allow eating while bridled.

attachment, a bar that runs vertically and spreads out pressure to help prevent the bit ring from pulling through the colt's mouth. Before riding the colt we'll have done groundwork, teaching impulsion by free-longing and the many typical steps involved in getting him used to grooming, handling feet (including leading by each foot as discussed earlier), and becoming comfortable with the saddle. I am a great believer in ground driving with long reins. The first time or two we'll drive with reins attached to halter alone, and then, when we're fairly sure the colt understands pressure well enough that he won't bolt and hurt his mouth, we'll switch to driving with the snaffle.

The ground driving lets us teach several basics, including "whoa" (the most important verbal cue you can teach a horse), "back," and simple turning in each direction, always remembering to give with one rein what we've taken away with the other. I also like to tie a colt back with one rein to the cinch ring on a saddle, but I don't defeat the purpose by cramming him around tightly, his neck bent in a curve. There's no pressure/release involved in doing that—the colt gets no reward for doing the right thing. Instead I tie one rein to the cinch ring in a way that just takes the slack out of the rein and nudges him slightly in the direction of a turn that way. Now he teaches himself. He finds that bending his neck just a little more relieves him of the pressure of the rein. Now, we repeat the process on the other side. A few minutes per side of this before each training session does wonders in building toward direct reining and that eventual one-rein stop.

Ground driving a colt. Here a riding saddle is used with reins through the stirrups, which should be tied together under the horse's belly. The author prefers using a sawbuck packsaddle.

I often use a sawbuck packsaddle rather than a riding saddle or bitting rig for ground driving. The sawbuck is light and handy, and like all packsaddles, it features a breeching that fits under the tail, good training should I eventually decide to ride with a crupper. Another advantage of using the packsaddle is that it's relatively easy to hang two soft panniers on the saddle, secured underneath with the necessary strap, as these further the colt's experience with things that make noise and clutter his rearward vision. Even better, weight can be added to the panniers to give the colt his first experience with the weight to come. Indeed, we've started many saddle horses by training them as packhorses first, and it works remarkably well. I've ponied many colts up onto our east range carrying a sack of salt for the cattle in each pannier.

Nothing so far has anything to do with the neck rein, but that's coming soon. Determining when the colt is ready to ride is an art in itself, but suffice it to say he should be thoroughly used to the sound and feel of the saddle, should be comfortable with our standing in the stirrup on each side, and he should be responsive enough to rein pressure on each side that we're quite sure we can bring him around if necessary.

We've also prepared the colt in another way that looks forward to cueing with the legs. From the ground I press my knuckles or the handle of a curry into the colt's side as a signal to move away from the pressure. There are many systems of leg cues, but at this point I'm most interested in a cue fairly far forward, up toward the front cinch, and I want the colt to move away from it.

So the scene is set. Enough groundwork has been done that we judge the colt to be ready to ride. Our preparation isn't foolproof, however—things can happen, so we'll be careful. It's very rare that our colts try to buck on the first ride. A few have a startle reaction, which we control by bringing them around into a tight circle, but that is rare. It's far more common for the colt to stand in one place, a little perplexed at the feel of weight on his back.

Petting on the neck helps soothe the colt, and perhaps it's fine to get off at this point and call it a first ride, even though the colt went nowhere. But usually we take up slack on one rein, cue the horse forward, and get him to move. A circle or two each way around the round pen certainly constitutes a successful first ride. And it's on this very first ride that we begin teaching the neck rein.

Every time I turn the colt I give him three signals. For a left turn I give direct rein pressure with the left rein. But I also make sure to lay the right rein on the right side of his neck, and I also press my right heel into his side at approximately the cinch line. It's easiest to remember this by thinking of push-pull. The left rein pressure is pull, while the right rein on the colt's neck and the right heel pressed into his side are push. When you turn right, you reverse the procedure.

Although I normally prefer light split reins, I find it helpful to use a one-piece (loop) rein of heavier leather on these early rides. (Some trainers prefer the rope reins currently in vogue.) A heavier rein is easier for the colt

Three cues are given each time the colt is asked to turn—direct rein in direction of turn, neck rein on off side of neck, and leg cue forward on off side of torso with the leg in the direction of turn relieving any pressure.

to feel as it lies on his neck. When the time comes for split reins, I begin working as much as possible with one hand, holding fingers between the reins in such a way that I can give subtle inside (direct) rein as needed. I've had clients express surprise that it's okay to put fingers between the reins when holding them in one hand. When I ask why it shouldn't be, they usually cite judging in a show class that prohibits it. I explain that such regulations only exist so that judges have criteria to deduct points. In the backcountry you are the judge. Your success, your safety, and your pleasure are the trophies.

You'll find yourself better in tune with the horse if your rein hand is relatively close to the horse's neck, in front of the pommel with just six inches to a foot of space between your hand and the neck. Too often I see riders holding the reins with one hand up at chest (or even chin) level. Mechanically, this position is counterproductive. The long distance between the horse's bit and your hand tends to keep the rein pressing almost vertically past his neck. A closer spacing tends to wrap the rein on the "push" side across the top of the neck, a more obvious cue. Similarly, shortening the hand position better allows that subtle bit of inside (direct rein) pressure should it be needed.

Consistently giving all three of these cues—direct rein, neck rein, and leg cue—each time you turn the horse eventually leads to the time you can eliminate one and eventually two of them, leaving only the neck rein. Many of us apply the same principle when training our dogs, scarcely giving it a thought. My younger Airedale started jumping into the pickup after some coaxing on the command "Load," accompanied by an arm gesture. Soon there was no need for the verbal command, just the arm gesture. Now merely a slight flick of my wrist does the trick.

With a colt (or older horse) learning to neck rein, the direct rein is the first cue I try to eliminate. I begin accompanying the neck rein only with the leg cue. When he's solid in this regard, I begin to neck rein only. If he forgets, it's easy to return to these earlier cues. But it's important not to return to the direct rein too readily. Be a little bit stubborn. If the colt hesitates to turn, give him a moment. Put more pressure into the leg cue.

Although I rarely wear spurs in the backcountry, I do like them for this early training. As mentioned above, spurs aren't my first choice for teaching or enforcing impulsion. A slap on the rear tends to be more effective for that. But spurs allow isolation of leg cues because the pressure they exert is more precise, less generalized than that of a whole heel or leg. Spurs should be used gently, and there's no need for harsh or sharp rowels. I've often found that just a light touch with a spur is more effective than considerable pressure applied with leg and heel.

On a horse already trained to neck rein, responsiveness can be hurt by a rider who quickly reverts to direct reining. This can happen when an impatient rider rushes at the slightest delay in turning to reach down and pull one rein. After a day carrying such a rider, one of my old reliable geldings became confused enough that he lost some of his finely tuned neck rein. He'd begun to wait for that tug on the rein that hadn't been needed before. Thankfully, a ride or two straightened out his confusion.

I emphasize in clinics that before the horse will neck rein, you, the rider, must neck rein! Often I have clinic clients spend a half hour or so negotiating various obstacles set up in the arena. Then I ask them to put one of their hands in a pocket and continue. They have a jump start on success, because their horses have already encountered the obstacles. Many find the experience challenging at first, but it's amazing how quickly the horses pick up on the cues and begin to handle well when guided by just one hand. Then

For the horse to neck rein, you must neck rein. A good technique for self-discipline is to put one hand in your pocket.

I add another step by handing riders the lead rope of another horse and asking them to pony it through the obstacles.

The horse that's spent his life carrying riders in English style may present a challenge, but often can be converted to the neck rein without too much difficulty. I've known riders from the Midwest who believe that to accomplish that change the reins should be crossed under the neck. The theory is that a horse so rigged will feel a tug on the left rein when a neck rein is applied on the right. Although I've met people who swear by this approach, I've never seen any need for it.

On the English horse, go back to basics, returning to the snaffle if necessary. Do what you can to encourage the horse to relax. From the ground, practice cueing the horse. Mounted, ask him to bend toward the direct pressure you exert. Then, ride just as you would a colt with the three cues we've discussed—the direct rein, neck rein, and leg cue simultaneously. It's likely the horse will be used to turning to direct rein pressure, so in a sense that's a head start.

Now work with the reins in one hand, with your knuckles between the reins so you can "cheat" a little. As you neck rein, turn your hand to give a

Help a rancher move cattle to build a neck rein.

bit of inside rein as well and remember the leg cue. Most horses will adjust and pick it up quickly.

"Finishing" the rein on most of my horses comes beyond the round pen. Following other horses on the trail, make sure you neck rein at each twist and turn in the trail, even though your horse would follow the one in front of him without any cue at all. The constant repetition, the constant feel, of the rein on his neck accompanied by the natural impulse to turn, builds the habit you're after. And really, training is mostly a matter of instilling habits you desire while preventing the rise of those you don't.

If you know a rancher who needs help moving cattle, offer to help— that activity builds a neck rein rapidly. The constant need to weave first left, then right, going back and forth all day while following a herd of cows is wonderful training. Helping a neighbor each spring and fall to move a herd back and forth to his summer range, I several times rode out in the morning with a snaffle-bitted colt that hadn't a clue about neck reining and brought back that evening a horse with a silky neck rein.

A word to the wise, however, about working cattle: do make sure you have what cowboys call a good "handle" on your horse before volunteering

Cutting cows in close quarters requires a good neck rein.

to help. Again in cowboy vernacular, things can get a little "western" when you gallop to head off a straggler that's headed in the wrong direction.

Riding across open sagebrush flats off trail is wonderful practice for the neck rein. Having no trail to follow, the horse becomes totally reliant on you to show him the best way through. You'll pick a path to the right, then one to the left, going back and forth as you progress. The horse will feel for your cues. And if you happen to live where sagebrush flats don't exist, riding off trail over any relatively flat area can accomplish the same thing. Keep the horse guessing as to which way you want to go, then turn him with the neck rein.

At a certain point I switch from the snaffle to a mild curb bit such as what's commonly called a grazing bit. Yes, some folks keep their horses in the snaffle indefinitely. That can be okay if you're pleased with the horse's handling and he's responsive to the neck rein. But it's important to remember that the snaffle is a direct rein bit and it isn't particularly comfortable for the horse when pressured back with one hand on both reins.

On most curb bits I adjust the curb strap or chain so that it doesn't engage (press) onto the lower jaw until the shanks are pulled back several inches. Often an adjustment that allows you to easily insert a couple of fingers under the strap is just about right. This helps build lightness, because the horse learns to respond to the first touch of pressure, avoiding the tug of the bit that results from a firmer touch.

Usually I observe an uptick in the horse's progress toward the neck rein when I switch to a mild curb. Just when in training I make the switch depends on that progress, but also on his general behavior and disposition. What's the likelihood that this particular horse will spook and try to buck or bolt? Has he progressed to the point when need for the one-rein stop is unlikely?

The snaffle, the bit with which the horse has been initially trained, works somewhat better for the one-rein stop, because pull on one rein tends to be isolated from the other side of the bit, assuming you remember to give slack on the off side. Also, during training, you should have practiced endlessly bending the horse left and right in turn. The curb bit, on the other hand, tends to generalize the pull on one rein, so that in effect, the horse feels some pull on both sides, even though only one rein is pressured.

I normally adjust the curb strap to allow a couple of fingers to slide in easily.

That said, the one-rein stop isn't completely unavailable after the switch is made, as some have claimed. A reasonably strong individual in a tight situation who pulls on one side of the horse's bit can still bring him around, particularly if the horse has been trained to give in one direction. It's just that the snaffle is a bit more efficient in this regard.

Although it's hard to generalize, I tend to switch to a mild curb when the horse is steady on the neck rein about 50 to 75 percent of the time. In other words, I get the turning response I wish more than half the time without either of the two additional cues. At this stage, the need for direct rein is pretty much gone, and only an occasional leg cue is needed to reinforce the neck rein. But there's no need to be rigid on this point. Returning to the snaffle is just fine if you feel any backslide, and I often do so when teaching the side pass, our next concern.

And why the side pass? Isn't that only a dressage maneuver, something on which to be judged in a horse show? Hardly. Let's envision a mountain trail, a somewhat scary one of the type featured in one particular valley near my home. The trail at one point is a ledge. There's a cliff on the right dropping straight down perhaps a hundred feet. On the left is a wall, the upper part of the cliff, pure granite garnished with green moss where trickles of springwater run across it.

The trail has been blasted out of the cliff with dynamite, probably back during the 1930s, and it's adequately wide, at least six feet across. But your horse is one of those that insists on walking close to the edge, perhaps enjoying the view. Knowing that even sure-footed horses are fallible, we're nervous about that. Rockytop, one of my first geldings, tall and long necked, was of that type. He liked nothing better than craning his neck over the edge to see what was beyond the next bend. I, his rider, didn't care for that at all.

Yes, we can rein this overly brave beast to our left away from the edge, but when we turn his front end to the left, his rear end tends to swivel to the right, toward the edge, not what we want at all. We want to be able to press the whole horse, not just one end of him, away from the edge back in toward the security of the rock wall. And that's why the backcountry horse needs to be trained to side pass. As a skill it's also handy for such tasks as opening gates.

In teaching the neck rein, you've already performed the groundwork necessary for the side pass. My approach isn't very sophisticated, but it works. Return to two-handed riding initially, with the snaffle if necessary. Spend some time on the ground next to your horse, renewing his response to pressure around the middle of his torso, pushing him away from you. He's probably already used to your moving him this way, perhaps with the command, "Over."

Let's start with a side pass to my left. Riding along an arena fence or wall to my right, I change the angle, turning toward the wall first at about 45 degrees. The horse anticipates a turnaround to my right, but I don't let him go any farther in that direction. Keeping his forward momentum if I can, I angle him toward the wall just a little more steeply and keep his head reined straight while cueing him with my right leg and firmly saying, "Pass!" As he feels the cue on his right side, trained as he is to this point, he'll try to turn left, but with the reins I'll prevent him from doing so. Applying sharp cues from my right leg, being careful not to pressure with my left, I try to get him to take a sideways step or two.

That's how it begins. I'm not above cheating a little. Within our indoor arena, the hitching rail lies just outside the main gate into the riding ring. Horses think of that hitching rail as home and are always eager to return there. I'll often side-pass first toward that gate from one direction or the other. That adds to the motivation.

All we're after in the beginning is a sideways step or two. At first, we're getting the horse to translate his forward momentum into a sideways step.

Begin the sidepass by angling in toward the wall.

Translate momentum into sideways movement by not allowing the horse to turn—continue to leg cue him in the direction you wish to go while saying "Pass!"

Then we'll begin stopping the horse away from the wall, applying the leg cues while holding his head straight, saying, "Pass." Once he understands that in this particular case he's not being asked to move either forward or back, he'll begin to respond as we wish. Eventually, after much practice, you'll get that light-touch pass in either direction, and you'll have less to fear from that stargazing horse that likes to look over the edge at the "view."

Patience is key, because we're asking the horse to do something that's a bit unnatural for him. With a rider aboard, the horse is used to forward and backward movement, not sideways, and it takes a while for him to understand what we're asking. Physically he's certainly capable of it, though. One of the nicest side passes I ever executed in front of an audience was totally unintended, by a horse not yet trained for it, but people watching were unaware of that.

My wife, Emily, and I were riding in a small-town parade. I didn't belong on a horse at all, because my left leg hadn't fully recovered from a ski accident that fractured my fibula. I could only mount from the right side by holding on to the saddle horn to relieve the left leg of weight while I got my right foot into the stirrup. The fact that the black gelding I was riding that day stood taller than sixteen hands was no help at all.

Then the parade marshal, oblivious to the needs of equestrians, placed Emily and me directly behind a lodge's "Oriental Band," men dressed in Middle Eastern costumes, playing exotic (and very noisy) instruments. This was a sight our horses hadn't seen before, and they eyeballed the men with suspicion, showing the whites of their eyes. Once underway we did okay until the first intersection on Main Street, when the band stopped to play.

With a fire truck behind and the squawking Oriental Band in front, my horse had nowhere to go. Too well behaved to buck or run away, he instead executed a perfect side pass starting on the left side of the paved street, crossing the center stripe, and stopping only when he reached the spectators on my right. I did my best to look cool throughout, and I must have succeeded, because a ripple of applause went through the folks in the crowd, who thought the side pass was intentional. Luckily, at that point, the

Opening and closing a gate with the horse pressed sideways against it can be good practice for the sidepass.

band moved forward. The next time they stopped to play, Emily and I managed to scoot around them. I was reminded of the man who remodeled our kitchen and told me the mark of a good carpenter was how well he covered up his mistakes. I'd managed to get away with something similar.

So the side pass, while initially unfamiliar to the horse, is well within his physical capability. Practicing by opening swinging gates can be helpful. Pressure your horse toward the gate with leg cues. Anxious to walk out of it when opened, he'll probably want to face the gate, but be stubborn and you'll eventually get him to stand parallel to it. Grasp the gate (unlatched in advance, if necessary) and cue the horse so that the gate moves with you, either toward you or away from you. Then reverse the direction. The horse soon understands the gate is to move with him, either pushing or pulling. You're not only refining the side pass, you're teaching your horse a valuable skill that will save dismounting and mounting out in the field, something that becomes even more helpful as you age!

Working with the gate requires use of just one hand on the reins, an ideal preamble to your ultimate goal. A seamless side pass first in one direction, then the other, with the rider holding the reins in one hand and scarcely moving them is a beautiful thing to watch.

CHAPTER SIX

WALK ON: IMPROVING THE MOST IMPORTANT BACKCOUNTRY GAIT

A "finished" horse (a bit of a misnomer, since training should continue throughout a horse's life) should work in all gaits, should lope in figure-eight patterns, and should be as tractable and responsive as a good sports car. However, those accomplishments, important as they are in other areas, matter far less in the backcountry. The backcountry horse will spend the bulk of his time in one gait, the walk. But all walks aren't the same, and since this gait is the basic one we'll be using "back there" we should do what we can to improve it.

And most modern saddle horses really need improvement in this area. Indeed, if there's any gait that's been allowed to lapse in importance, it's the walk (except in gaited breeds, which we'll discuss later). As teenagers looking for deer, my brother and I walked up a ridge watching a pair of horse back hunters working their way up a parallel ridge. We found we moved considerably faster than the two on horseback, and I decided then and there that I wasn't interested in any horse that walked more slowly than I do.

Peruse the show classes of America's largest horse breed and you won't find a single class that rewards the sort of snappy, ground-covering walk our forefathers demanded of their horses. Worse, you'll find a class called "Western Pleasure" that rewards a snail's-pace walk, the animal's head down toward the dirt, its butt in the air, looking, in the words of my cowboy father-in-law, "Like it's ashamed of itself." The same class features a "trot" equally pokey and a "canter" (lope) so slow and bound up that the horses look lame. There is nothing either western or pleasurable about a horse that moves in that fashion.

Although rough country and rocky trails may limit our horses to the walking gait, that doesn't mean it has to be slow. Variable, yes—the backcountry horse must walk slowly when asked to pony packhorses across a creek or when the trail is truly treacherous, but he should speed up to a snappy walk of around four miles per hour or better when we hit the smooth portions of the trail. Today our cell phones contain GPS apps that measure speed. I use one called "Backcountry Navigator." Set your phone to the appropriate setting and ask your horse to walk out. If he's of a nongaited breed and breaks to a trot at less than four miles per hour, he is not walking up to potential, and your back feels it. You have work to do.

The walk has two features in common among all breeds of horses that make it the most comfortable gait. First, it's a four-beat gait, with every foot hitting the ground separately, and it's accompanied by a nod of the head that disappears when the animal breaks into a trot. One way to look at the footfall sequence of the walk is right-front, left-rear, left-front, right-rear. Because each foot hits separately, shock is spread out. Physiologists claim that the footfall pattern actually makes the walk therapeutic for the rider's back.

The walk's other outstanding feature is sure-footedness. The trot is a suspension gait. Left-front and right-rear hooves hit simultaneously, then right-front and left-rear. Between these two pairs of concussion there's a moment of suspension in which the horse is out of contact with the ground. At the walk, however, three of four feet are on the ground (or just touching or just leaving it) at any one time. Football coaches frequently ask their defensive players to take short, choppy steps. The idea is to maintain contact with the ground so a player will not be "faked out" while he's in the air (suspension). A horse's walk has the same advantage, because it keeps him in contact with the ground, a safety plus.

Equine physiologist Dr. Deb Bennett has said that all horses are physically capable of walking six miles per hour. So why, as I've often observed, do many of today's horses, particularly those of "stock horse" build, break to a trot at two or three miles per hour? Quite simply, it's because they've been allowed to. With little incentive to walk better, with riders who don't realize the horse need not trot at slow speed, and with uses that involve more miles riding on highways in horse trailers than in covering ground, some horses have simply become accustomed to breaking into a slow jog. There's probably nothing inherently wrong with this if the horse's trot is relatively smooth (for a trot) or if you don't mind posting. To me the idea of posting in the backcountry is anathema.

Some years ago while working on a magazine article on this subject, we timed walking speed with GPS using some of our Tennessee Walking Horses, several Quarter Horse mares owned by a neighbor, and my little miniature horse Razzy. The Walking Horses, even when held to an ordinary walk (not a flat walk or running walk) all moved along at more than four miles per hour, aided by their long steps and overstride. The Quarter Horse mares initially wanted to trot at around two-and-a-half to three miles per hour.

Razzy was the surprise. His little legs moving in a blur, but still in a walk, not a trot, he easily topped four miles per hour. To do so he had to step twice as fast as the mares, but he did so, and from our experiences with him while pulling a cart, we knew he could keep up that speed for a long stretch.

Perhaps motivated by Razzy's performance, the owner of the Quarter Horse mares, an excellent horseman and trainer, tried a simple experiment. He rode each of the mares at a walk, gradually speeding up, but not letting the horse break into a trot. Just at the point he felt the shift to a trot occur, he'd rein in, then repeat the process. The results were amazing.

Razzy, a miniature horse, walked an honest four miles per hour.

Within an hour each mare was giving him a solid four-mile-per-hour walk—and it was simply because the rider had emphasized it and demanded it.

The walk can often be improved by a mixture of impulsion and collection. Merely sitting on a horse's back with drooping reins tells the animal it can laze along. "To ride," after all, is an active verb, at least when it pertains to horses. The rider is not a mere passenger. I recall my father-in-law mounting a nondescript pinto mare that when standing in the field conveyed no sense of pride or animation. But when Elmer put his foot in the stirrup, swung on, and sat squarely on her back, the mare came alive. Her neck arched; her whole manner changed. A horseman had mounted her, and she sensed there would be expectations.

Insist that your horse walk out boldly, and if it offers to trot without giving you a snappy walk, rein back, but continue to squeeze your legs. If necessary go back to lunging, but not at a trot. Command "Walk!' bringing him back down to that gait as necessary, but keeping him moving, head nodding and carried no lower than his withers.

Some horses will pick up their walk while following another horse that steps out, but that will only work if your friend ahead is sympathetic to your needs. Ideally the lead horse will slow down if necessary, keeping the speed within your horse's capability but right at the top end of his walking speed. Keeping up with the horse in front might supply some of impulsion he lacks when alone, which combined with a snug rein, may do the trick.

Gaited horse owners with pacey horses sometimes have success breaking the gait back into a walk by riding on soft footing such as a plowed field. I haven't tried this with a nongaited horse that's too quick to trot, but I suspect it may work, because horses are very aware of their footing and gravitate toward the walk when worried about slipping. Again, keep the horse moving smartly, but within the margins of safety. Don't let him saunter.

Improving the walk of gaited horses calls for a similar approach, but first some background is in order. The term "gaited" is a little misleading, since all horses have gaits, normally encompassing the walk, the trot, and the canter or lope (which becomes a gallop at high speed). As mentioned above, the walk is a four-beat gait and the trot a two-beat gait. The canter is actually a three-beat gait. On the right lead it starts with the left hind leg, then the right hind and left front leg hitting simultaneously, all followed by the right hind leg.

But nature has bestowed on certain equines a set of extra "gears." Current research suggests that all gaited horses probably descended from one ancestor with a gait mutation. Humans, enjoying the improved ride, then bred for this gait variation. This probably occurred eons ago, because gaited breeds are spread far and wide, from Mongolia to Iceland to the British Isles and to the Americas, where they probably descended from a Spanish breed called the "jennet," brought by the early explorers. The late trainer and clinician Lee Ziegler, in her book *Easy Gaited Horses*, identified more than seventy gaited breeds worldwide.

Interestingly, the great shift in way of going centered on a gait that in itself isn't particularly desirable for a saddle horse, though very useful in harness. The mother gait of gaited animals is the pace, a two-beat gait but the direct opposite of the trot. Instead of diagonally opposed legs (left-front and right-rear) hitting simultaneously, both legs on one side of the horse land together when the animal paces. This makes for a side-to-side motion that is not particularly comfortable. Ask anyone who has ridden a camel— they are hard pacers.

But the pace as a mother gait opens up a whole treasure chest of four-beat gaits, faster than the walk, more comfortable than the trot, and wonderful to ride. The most basic of these is the amble, which is the most common gait among gaited breeds worldwide. In the amble, sometimes called the stepping pace or the saddle gait, the pace is broken into four beats. The left rear hits first, then the left front, followed by the right rear and the right front. Chaucer in his *Canterbury Tales* mentions that the Wife of Bath sits comfortably on an ambling horse. A somewhat pampered character, this woman would have insisted on a comfortable horse.

The "extra gears" found in gaited horses fall along a spectrum between two extremes, the two-beat diagonal trot at one end, and the pace, a two-beat lateral gait, at the other. The foxtrot leans toward the diagonal, while the flat walk and running walk (sometimes called "square gaits") fall in the middle, and the amble, stepping pace, and the several paso gaits, along with a host of other variations, all fall toward the lateral end of the spectrum. In all of these you'll hear four distinct hoofbeats while riding, but in the flat walk and running walk you'll hear these four hoofbeats in even time (think musical quarter notes in 4/4 time), while in most of the others you'll hear two closer together, a slight pause, then the other two hitting singly.

The advantage of all these gaits, the quality which made them so popular worldwide, is smoothness-at-speed. Any horse is relatively smooth to ride when it saunters. The beauty of the flat walk, running walk, foxtrot, tölt, and amble is that they allow a rider to progress at trot speed, but since concussion is broken into four parts rather than two, enjoying greater comfort in the saddle.

The historical ebb and flow in popularity of gaited breeds has been directly related to the building of roads passable to wheeled vehicles. Smooth gaits were not particularly important once most travel was by buggy or wagon—the wheeled vehicle was equally smooth (or not) regardless of the horse's gait. But in areas where the growth of civilization outstripped the building of roads and infrastructure, gaited breeds remained popular. The American South, Iceland, and parts of South America were among the regions where horseback travel continued to be the norm until just a century or so ago. When the first automobile to arrive in Iceland was put on exhibit in Reykjavik during the early twentieth century, there was no road on which it could be driven. There were only trails, even within the city, so the car could not be demonstrated. All travel then was still undertaken by foot and horseback on the hardy little Icelandic horses with their fast tölt gaits.

In the United States, however, infrastructure had improved so much by the early twentieth century that gaited breeds fell out of favor. In earlier years horses were ridden to a horse show or branding, but now horses could be transported to the occasion by horse trailer, and smoothness and endurance became less important. Performance within arenas became the emphasis of breeding and training.

Today, though, trail riding and backcountry use have become the number one activity for equestrians, and gaited breeds are again mushrooming in popularity. Some years ago I gave a presentation at the state convention of Montana Backcountry Horsemen and asked how many in the audience rode gaited animals. Only a smattering raised their hands. A decade later I was asked to speak again, and this time nearly half the audience indicated they were riding gaited animals.

Among those who haven't ridden them, gaited horses still suffer from some unfortunate stereotypes. One is that they're unsuitable for rough country, prone to stumbling. But this directly conflicts with history, for it's in rough, unsettled country that they were always preferred. Unfortunately, some gaited breed organizations have favored shoeing with long toes to create greater action (lift) of the front hooves, a great detriment to backcountry sure-footedness. Gaited horses should be shod like any other breed for tough terrain. It's true, too, that gaited breeds tend to tempt riders to go too fast on dangerous terrain. Some trails are unsafe at any but the slowest speeds regardless of gait.

Some gaited breeds, the Tennessee Walking Horse in particular, have received a black eye for an extreme, unnatural, and in the eyes of some, inhumane show tradition that includes the so-called "big lick." Horses with padded front hooves are exhibited in an unnatural, exaggerated gait, as alien to the way a horse should freely move as the western pleasure classes within the Quarter Horse breed on the opposite end of the spectrum. Unfortunately, to the public, this may mask the fact that plain-shod walking horses are one of the most popular and capable breeds used in the backcountry. Most owners of this wonderful breed consider the big-lick show tradition to be alien and ugly.

Such abuses have led some to believe that these extra "gears" exhibited by gaited horses are artificial, created through training rather than breeding. But no training regime can put what's been called the "gait-keeper gene" into a horse. The ancient Romans gave it a try when they conquered the British Isles and envied the native horses ambling smoothly along. Engineers that they were, the Roman soldiers constructed wicked cross-chains to be worn by Barb horses in an attempt to break up the trot and make them "gaited." I suspect the result was cruel for the horse and not too successful for the rider.

Conformation and training can contribute to gaitedness, but neither can create it. One of our best broodmares could pass for a Quarter Horse, even under educated scrutiny, until you see her and her foals move out. The dead-natural barefoot running walk is there in a mare that's never even been broke to ride. Of course, good riding and training can enhance gait. We'll touch on that shortly.

Finally, there are those who are concerned about style and believe that gaited animals aren't "western." Again, historically this is inaccurate. The American West was populated by many breeds of horses, many of which were gaited. Among mustangs a silver pacing stallion became the stuff of legend in the days Washington Irving was writing about the West. A magnificent animal that was never caught, the stallion and others like him must have done their part to sire gaited genetics within the free-roaming horses of the Great Plains. My wife's grandfather bought untouched horses from the Crow tribe in south-central Montana, and he was always able to find a "single-footer" among them to keep for himself.

Among writers of the West, there's no better authority on the sort of horses found in the Dakotas and eastern Montana during the cowboy years than our twenty-sixth president, Theodore Roosevelt. Roosevelt went west in the early 1880s first to hunt, then to find a new life after his heart was broken by the deaths of his wife and mother at his house from separate illnesses on the very same day. Purchasing a cattle ranch, Roosevelt threw himself into the world of the cowboy and took many of the knocks associated with hard riding over rough terrain. During that time gaitedness, often generalized in the term "single-foot," was the norm, not the exception, among the horses he encountered.

In *Hunting Trips of a Ranchman*, one of his many writings from this period, Roosevelt mentions approaching some grouse that he covets for dinner. Believing he'd be more likely to spook them on foot, he instead nears them on horseback "at the regular cow-pony gait—a kind of single-foot pace, between a walk and a trot."

Roosevelt's cattle ran on two ranches forty miles apart, and a ride between the two locations was a simple afternoon affair on these smooth, fast-moving horses. In *The Wilderness Hunter* Roosevelt adds detail about the way such horses moved and what the cowboys of the time preferred:

> My foreman and I rode beside the wagon on our wiry, unkempt, unshod cattle-ponies. They carried us all day at a rack, pace, single-foot, or slow lope, varied by rapid galloping when we made long circles after game; the trot, the favorite gait with eastern park-riders, is disliked by all peoples who have to do much of their life-work in the saddle.

Certainly my affection for the gaited breeds shows through, and it's based on a lifetime of use managing my cattle, taking me to the mountains, and carrying my children. But all is not gravy. As with other breeds, sloppy riding keeps many of the animals from reaching their potential.

Most gaited horses naturally progress in an easy ordinary walk that is deceptively fast, often because the animal overstrides. The horse's hind leg reaches farther forward than the track of the front foot on the same side. With these longer steps, the horse can seem to be idling along while the nongaited animal next to him must trot. So far so good.

But since most gaited horses are actually multigaited, it's easy for the lackadaisical rider to nullify some of their advantages by letting the horse get lazy. Just as the nongaited animal might adopt the habit of breaking to a trot at walking speed, gaited horses sometimes gravitate to a pace when they should be at flat-walk or foxtrot speed. The pace is not inherently comfortable—it's a two-beat gait like the trot—and it's not a good rough-terrain gait because of that moment of suspension between footfalls. The left front and rear hit the ground, and then there's a moment of suspension before the right feet come down.

A friend of mine outfitted in the Bob Marshall Wilderness of western Montana for many years using Tennessee Walking Horses exclusively. I stood next to him while we watched light-shod show classes. Some of the horses were doing nice flat walks and running walks, but many were pacing. "Notice," he said, "that most of those pacing horses are moving along with drooping reins and their noses sticking out—and their riders have smiles on their faces and don't even realize that their horses aren't walking."

Similarly, watching a television show featuring horses on the trail, I saw riders pass by on a variety of gaited horses, and at least half were pacing, the riders' bodies rocking side to side, the sounds of their hooves as they passed the video camera completely lacking that nice 4/4 time that comes with a smooth ground-covering gait. And, as my friend had observed, most of the horses progressed on completely slack reins. The people mounted on these horses were passengers, not riders.

Since Xenophon, collection has been a key ingredient in nearly all horse disciplines. Basically, the term refers to shortening the horse, bringing his body into a more compact unit so that the back rounds and the power comes from his hindquarters which push him, rather than his forequarters "pulling" him. Books have been written on the subject, so this, obviously, is an oversimplification.

To have collection, you must have impulsion. The horse has to drive himself forward with his hind quarters. And, up front, there must be a certain amount of restraint. Gaited horses don't need (or deserve) the combination of impulsion and collection forced on them by extreme show trainers. To perform well in the flat walk, running walk, or foxtrot (depending on breed) they need not be forced into a high-leverage bit.

But some collection nearly always accompanies the gaits we're looking for in gaited animals. The pacey horse can be handled in the very same way my neighbor handled his Quarter Horse mares to make them walk better. Move the horse boldly forward, but keep it at a walk. A shift to the pace will be very obvious both in the way your body is treated and in the way the horse handles its head—it will stop nodding. Driving the horse forward, but limiting its speed when it attempts to break gait, will improve the regular walk. Then, if you want more speed, that good walk can gradually transition into the flat walk, running walk, or foxtrot (or, in the case of one of the Paso breeds) a rapid gait that stays four-beat and smooth.

Yes, it's all a bit more complicated than this, but you get the idea. Make your horse work. He's on duty when you ride him. It's also my firm belief that the horse used to working is also the safer horse, the more aware horse, the horse less likely to do something stupid, such as stepping off the side of a trail in a delicate spot.

There are also a few "old-timer" techniques to help the horse that breaks his walk to a pace and also the converse, the fairly common gaited animal that breaks to a trot rather than performing the four-beat gait we're after. These approaches don't involve corrective shoeing or the many "action devices," such as chains around the pasterns that may be unkind to the horse or in extreme cases—such as the soring of walking horses—abusive.

Pacey horses often respond well to being ridden on soft surfaces, such as snow or a farmed field. On such a surface, as on a rough backcountry trail, it's difficult for the animal to stay in the lock-step, two-beat pace, and he'll often work in the four-beat gait we desire, his instincts telling him the better gait is also the more sure-footed. Traveling on the soft surface also builds conditioning in the correct gait.

Working the pacey horse in a tight circle can also be successful. The circle makes the distance traveled by each side of the horse unequal. Cars have differentials to take care of this issue—on a tight turn the differential in the axle allows the wheel on the outside of the turn to rotate faster than that on the inside. Working a pacey horse in a tight circle has a similar effect—the horse will break the pace to better compensate for the different distances traveled by his right and left side, and that's what we're after.

Though one hears more about problems with the pacey horse, the trotty gaited horse can become an equally difficult problem. Trotty horses respond to surfaces exactly the opposite. They'll tend to give you the desired gait when ridden on a hard surface such as a paved road. Again, riding on the surface to which the animal best responds will tend to build the muscles for the gait you're after.

Most Tennessee Walking Horses and Fox Trotters are multigaited. Many can perform the flat walk, running walk, foxtrot, pace, trot, and amble. Limiting them to the gait you desire is part of training. I let a young gelding I'd ridden just a couple of times go to a trainer who owed me several colt starting sessions. It was against my better judgment, because the colt was coming along so well, but I was busy, and the person was completely trustworthy—I'd known him since childhood.

The gelding came back well-started, already neck reining, ready to go. But the running walk I'd noted since the horse was a new foal in the pasture with its dam was now completely gone. Once I pushed the horse past a slow walk, he trotted, and his trot was on the rough side. What I hadn't counted on was that this excellent trainer was a cowboy in orientation, and he was concerned with everything except gait, which he hardly noticed.

A Tennessee Walking Horse foal displays his bold, flat-footed walk. The "extra gears" of gaited horses are genetic, inborn.

I took the gelding to a clinic taught by a friend, where he was promptly kicked by another animal as we progressed around the arena. From then on he was hardly manageable in that setting, so worried as he was about being kicked again, that I took him outside onto the rodeo grounds where we could work alone. Charged up as he was, it took just a bit of collection and a few stern words, and he hit a beautiful running walk. He just had to find out what I wanted, and it was clear sailing from there.

In another case a friend sent a Peruvian Paso to a noted Quarter Horse trainer. When she went to pick up her horse the trainer commented, "I had a terrible time getting that horse to trot!" My friend went ballistic. She should have known, though, that the trainer simply wasn't accustomed to gaited breeds, that he didn't know she wanted to maintain her horse's excellent *paso* gaits.

Before you can improve a horse's walk, you have to know what your horse is doing. If you're displeased or if a gaited horse is rough when you push it up past a walk, you're not getting the gait you desire. An excellent clinician once viewed her clients riding their horses, then asked them to write down on a slip of paper what they thought their mount was doing and what they wanted improved. Many in the group thought their pacey horses were trotting, and vice versa. A good number believed their horses were performing a running walk, but were pacing instead. If necessary have a knowledgeable person watch you ride.

Having a video made, particularly if it can be shifted to slow motion, is especially helpful. You can then clearly see what's happening as each foot hits the ground. But one simple clue almost always applies. At the walk the horse will nod its head, and that nod will continue as it speeds to a flat walk, running walk, or foxtrot. If the nod completely disappears, the horse is probably pacing or trotting.

The backcountry horse exists to take us many miles, to be as kind to our backs as possible, given the terrain. There's no sense in owning a gaited animal unless you're reaping the benefits of what's being called the "gait keeper" gene.

CHAPTER SEVEN

WEIGHTY MATTERS: YOU AND YOUR GEAR ON THE HORSE'S BACK

If there's any particular requirement that distinguishes the mission of the backcountry horse from those of many of its equine cousins, it's the need to carry considerable weight over rough terrain. The jockey, usually a wisp of a person weighing around a hundred pounds, rides in a featherlight saddle so as not to impede the animal's singular purpose—to run fast. Eventing horses, jumpers, and even dressage horses operate with as little weight as possible on their backs. And, the women who participate in the event known as barrel racing fret about the gain of a pound or two, lest it impede their horse's performance.

It's only the backcountry horse that seems saddled with (too often, and I, too, am guilty) a heavy rider, his lunch, safety gear, and perhaps even enough equipment to accommodate an overnight stay. So how much can a horse safely carry?

Pose that question to many knowledgeable horsemen and you'll get an answer that is misleading at best, damaging at worst. The horseman is likely to say, "Twenty percent of its body weight." So you eyeball this muscular man or woman, look at his or her saddle, then at the horse favored, do the mental math, and unless you're polite and restrained you're likely to say, "Then you're overloading your horse every time you get on."

There's really only one correct answer to the question we've posed and that is, "It depends." Here's a brief list of the variables: conformation of the horse; condition of the horse; size of the horse; speed to be traveled; distance to be traveled; type of the terrain to be traveled, ability of the rider; distribution of weight on the horse's back; and saddle type and fit.

The "20 percent rule" is easy to debunk. Based on that guideline, a fat 1,200-pound horse would be able to carry more than the same horse slimmed down to 1,100 pounds. Of course, the opposite is true. The guideline is awkward in other respects as well. Few riders know what their horses weigh, although a weight tape can give a quick estimate.

Here are some general plusses and minuses regarding types of horses and their respective ability to carry weight. All comparisons are in the "all other things being equal" category, and all refer to percentage of body weight. Some may surprise you.

1. Small horses can carry a larger percentage of their weight than large horses. Yes, a 1,400-pound Part Draft can probably carry more than a 900-pound Arab, but not in terms of percentage of his weight. A 500-pound Welsh pony would outdo either one of them, again in terms of percentage.

2. Moderately muscled horses probably can carry more (again in terms of percentage) than heavily muscled horses. Muscle is heavy. If it exists for purposes other than weight carrying, such as ability to accelerate or turn quickly or to pull a plow, the heavy muscle is detrimental and weighs the horse down. You wouldn't bet on Mike Tyson as a marathon winner. His muscles exist for an entirely different purpose than endurance. During my time in the Marine Corps, I noticed that lean, but hard-muscled men did as well or better on forced marches carrying packs than stocky, heavily muscled Marines.

3. A short back is a plus, and that's simple physics. Put a board between two closely spaced chairs and you may be able to stand on it. Put the chairs farther apart and the board may bend or break.

4. A broad loin is one of the most important conformational assets a horse can have for carrying weight. Here's where many of the smaller breeds shine. Put your hand on your horse's back just behind the rib cage. Then slide it down on one side or the other while pressing firmly. Where the loin muscle ends you'll feel it drop off. The other side will be the same. The farther

Aided by her short back and broad loin, Tess handles the author's weight well, even in rough terrain.

Feeling for broad characteristic of horse's loin.

down the muscle extends, the better. This is the area of the back most vulnerable when the horse carries weight, and it's the area that requires a strong muscle to support the weight.

On a writing assignment in Iceland, I checked the loins of many of the horses at a stable I visited. The trainer asked what I was doing, and I explained. He seemed pleased at my conclusion that much of the Icelandic horse's ability to carry large individuals in a fast tölt over rough terrain was due to their extremely generous loin muscling.

Comparable in size and gait (and genetically related) are the horses of Mongolia, which are known to carry prodigious loads sometimes nearly equal to their own weight. I suspect they have extensive loins, though I've not had the chance to examine one. I'd note, too, unpleasant as the subject may be to some readers, that humans in both Iceland and Mongolia butcher a percentage of their horses for food. This makes for a very tough but very effective method of selective breeding or, if you prefer, natural selection. The horses that survive are the toughest, most able to serve their owners by performing under saddle.

Don't despair if the conformation of your favorite horse doesn't meet the above criteria in terms of back and loin. Any sound, well-conditioned horse can handle a reasonable amount of weight, and conditioning is the place to start. As the old-timers say, "A lean horse for a long pull." They were referring to draft animals, but the same applies to saddle horses. By lean we don't mean "poor." But the horse expected to carry a rider plus gear should not be weighed down by unnecessary fat. Unfortunately, halter classes in some breeds reward horses that are truly obese, equines that in hard use would never hold up. Those same old-time irreverent cowboys would probably ask owners of such horses if they were raising them to be sold by the pound, like fed steers.

Conditioning shouldn't wait until a week or so before a scheduled trip. Horses, like people, build strength by actually injuring their muscles, which causes soreness, then allows healing to take place; the muscles recover, and become stronger. To take your horse on a hard ride or two shortly before you head out for the backcountry simply means you'll be taking a horse that's sore. If serious weight loss is desired, start months in advance. If the horse is middle aged, he'll get in shape somewhat faster than the young horse. Young horses seem to need to start over in the conditioning process, if their exercise has been allowed to lapse, because they haven't built the muscle mass they'll have in maturity.

And it's wise to remember that horses are not fully mature until around age six. Younger horses can certainly go to the backcountry, but their loads should be lighter.

Progressively longer rides over the sort of terrain you'll be traveling in the backcountry are the best preparation, because that other variable in answering the question, "How much can he carry" is the combination of distance, speed, and terrain. In computing how much cargo their pack mules could handle, the US Army developed exacting criteria, published on charts that factored speed, distance covered per day, the type of terrain (cross country and hilly versus good roads and trails), and number of consecutive days the mules could handle a given load. The pack mules were all very similar in size, weight, and conditioning, fitting prescribed Army specifications. A normal load was 250 pounds, which the mules could be expected to carry twenty-five miles per day every day year-round, or fifteen miles per day in rough country, with no rest days required as long as the back remained free of sores. Since these mules weighed between 950 and 1,020 pounds, they were carrying around 25 percent of their weight.

As loads, distance, and speed increased, the number of consecutive days decreased. The charts progress to very heavy loads, weights with which we wouldn't burden our animals today, but with fewer consecutive days prescribed. The speeds on the chart are quite impressive, normally five or six miles per hour. These would suggest a very fast walk or a trot.

So while you may not be able to control your favorite horse's build, you can control his condition and your expectations in terms of distance covered, speed, and terrain. The other thing you can control is the way weight on his back is distributed. Where on his back does the weight least bother him? Where does it hamper him the most?

Horses, like humans and automobiles, have a center of gravity. Founder of the Equine Studies Institute in Livingston, California, Dr. Deb Bennett outlines a method for finding this using a photograph, copy machine, and heavy paper to create a silhouette of your horse, then a sort of pinwheel that allows approximation of your horse's center of gravity, since it will vary from horse to horse. But usually the center of gravity is fairly far forward, not far behind the front cinch of a full-rigged saddle, and is around a third of the way up its body.

Obviously, when we combine the weight of the horse with that of saddle, rider, and gear, the center of gravity alters. It can also alter at high speed, which is the reason jockeys ride with their weight so far forward. But for the horse's benefit, and for his weight-carrying ability, we wish to alter that center as little as possible. Bluntly put, that means we must keep weight forward. Weight to the rear or high into the air above the horse has a detrimental effect.

A student's answer when I asked her to draw a cartoon of the worst possible scenario for carrying gear on a saddle horse. The only thing she might have added would have been a pack on the rider's back! Courtesy of Whitney DeVilbiss Jacobs.

What does this say about huge saddlebags built more like packing panniers, intended for a complete array of camping gear for the rider who wants to camp out but doesn't wish to take a pack animal? And what does it say about something I'm seeing increasingly, particularly among hunters, the person who rides with a good-sized pack on his or her back?

First, the saddlebags: Years ago a friend built a beautiful pair of saddlebags for me out of heavy saddle skirting leather, complete with my brand tooled into their sides. I treasure these. That said, I've finally quit using them very often, because even when empty, they're heavy. The padded nylon bags that have gone with me recently are not as classy, but they're much lighter, and I believe every ounce of weight behind the saddle is detrimental to the horse.

Whether weight behind the saddle can actually damage kidneys, I can't say for sure. But it certainly rides right over the loin, the muscle upon which we're counting to support the load behind the rib cage. And it definitely rides well behind the horse's center of gravity.

I tell clients to avoid buying the most roomy saddlebags they can find. If you have space, you're likely to use it. If you were headed out on a trip and an airline official said you could bring a second bag free, you'd be likely to find something extra to take along whether you needed it or not. High capacity bags beg to be filled.

Earlier, we discussed uphill and downhill riding. Throwing your weight backward on either steep uphill slopes or steep downhill ones makes it harder for your horse to get his hind legs up under him. Excessive weight behind the saddle causes much the same problem. It's a safety hazard for another reason as well—it's easy to catch your leg on it when mounting and dismounting, which can be embarrassing at best, hazardous at worst.

In my earlier years as a backcountry horseman I sometimes went alone, without a packhorse, carrying a very minimum amount of camping gear on my saddle horse. I no longer do so, and I discourage it. Unless you're featherlight, adequate gear for you and your horse mounts up in weight quickly, and it's difficult to place it in a way that doesn't create difficulty for the horse and safety issues for you.

Yes, it can be done, and if you're a very light person it's a bit more feasible. But you must plan carefully and be concerned about every ounce. In addition to sticking with a bare minimum of gear, you'll take extra items for the horse, perhaps a picket line, hobbles, maybe a small bag of oats. The concept of going light and alone with only your saddle horse is even less feasible if it involves inclement or winter weather, which requires additional gear.

One thing you can do is to keep heavier items farther forward. Canteens, binoculars, and camera gear can fit in horn packs or hang on the front portion of the saddle. There's little worry you'll pull the center of gravity forward of the horse's own center—your body and saddle, situated behind the horse's center of gravity, take care of that issue.

As a young ranch hand, I was sometimes asked to pack salt to the cattle while riding a gelding named Tommy on what were supposed to be recreational rides with my bride-to-be. But my future father-in-law Elmer found ways to combine our fun with a useful task. He put two fifty-pound salt blocks into separate gunny sacks, then twisted the top of each sack, looped it over, and tied twine around the end and the "standing" part, thus creating a loop of cloth that fit over the saddle horn. So equipped, he placed both sacks, one hundred pounds in all, over the saddle horn, one on each side, on the horse I would ride to the hills.

At nineteen, in football shape, I weighed two hundred pounds. Add my clothing, thirty-five pounds of western saddle, then one hundred pounds of salt, and Tommy's load was at least 340 pounds. He was a stout part-Percheron weighing perhaps 1,200 pounds, but he was packing close to 30 percent of his weight. So the proper answer to "How much can he carry?" is, "It depends." In this case the variables favored his performing this task without injury.

First, the speed to the salt trough was slow, and the distance, about 1.5 miles, short. Secondly, the terrain was a ranch two-track which climbed around three hundred feet, a moderate backcountry grade on good footing. Third, Tommy would not have to repeat this the next day, since the cows only needed salt resupply every couple of weeks. Lastly, and perhaps most important, the weight was up front, and when combined with my own weight and that of the saddle, probably very close to his natural center of gravity. Elmer would not have dreamed of placing that kind of weight behind the saddle.

I am sometimes asked what I think about riding with a knapsack on one's back. My simple answer is "Don't do it!" Even the lightest day pack raises the center of gravity and throws it backward. That's the last thing you need. A heavy backpack seems to be increasingly allowed by hunting guides who like the hunter to be self-sufficient when he dismounts. But the result can be disastrous for both horse and hunter.

At a mountain camp, enjoying the morning while my partners looked for a mountain goat, I decided I'd been lazy enough and should do something for the benefit of the camp. We were low on drinking water—the nearly dried-up lake by which we had camped was so full of "wee beasties" that even filtered water wasn't an attractive thought. Knowing there was a spring a half mile down the trail, I loaded my saddlebags with canteens and bottles and headed down on Little Mack for some freshwater.

There was a dicey spot on the trail, a ledge of rock perhaps eighteen inches to two feet high, abrupt, like a step. On the way up to camp the previous evening this spot had posed no real problem for my athletic horse—he simply rose in front and gave a little hop. So I didn't worry about this minor obstacle while I filled canteens and stuffed them into my saddlebags. I added perhaps ten or fifteen pounds to the area behind the saddle.

Heading up trail we came to the same spot. Little Mack rose on his hind legs, preparing to give his little hop, when something strange and frightening occurred. He reached "top-dead-center," a point of balance on his hind legs. Terrifying thoughts of his tumbling over backward with my body underneath him on a rocky trail flashed through my mind in the split second of equilibrium. Leaning forward as far as I could, I grasped a wrist-sized tree branch with my right arm and pulled hard. Little Mack gave his anticipated hop up over the ledge, and all was well, or nearly so. I was scared out of my wits.

Whether Little Mack would have gone over backward is probably doubtful— he was a strong and athletic horse—and just how much the added weight in my saddlebags had to do with the situation, I can't measure. But I've never forgotten the incident.

When you ride with a pack on your back you're multiplying the chances of a wreck in a situation like I've described. And the high combined weight of your upper torso, your head, and the pack has incredible leverage that compounds the effect. Notice how easy it is to move a horse sideways when it comes too close to a tree, threatening injury to your leg. Reaching out, you push away on the tree, and your horse's body follows. This is because pushing so high up gives you tremendous leverage.

The same principle becomes a negative when your weight is centered high above the horse's back. Imagine the leverage you have with a long-handled wrench compared to a short one. The effect of weight up high on the horse's back is compounded with greater leverage, and that can pull the horse in a direction you don't desire. And in any case, any attempt at decent equitation is thoroughly shot down. Your riding will be sloppy and disconnected.

The backpack will also encourage you to lean back on downhill grades, making it harder for the horse to get his hind legs under him, as we discussed earlier. If you really must have so much gear with you that you're tempted to carry a pack on your back, consider adding a pack animal to your stable. (More on that later.)

Conditioning for weight-carrying is not the only concern. Your horse must be trained to tolerate pressure in unusual places, hear strange sounds, and encounter strange smells. His senses are much better than yours. The wind flapping the fold of that poncho rolled up behind the saddle may be an entirely new sound to the horse. Similarly, the extra equipment may affect the way you mount your horse.

So it's back to the principle of "try it first at home." Load up your gear, and don't be overly gentle about it. Make sure your horse knows what's there, knows the sound of your leg scraping the duffel bag tied behind the cantle. Long rides on familiar turf, fully loaded, will harden his muscles and his mind and pay dividends when you hit the wilderness trail.

There's one more thing most of us can do to help the horse carry weight, and it, too, involves conditioning. Many Americans can stand to drop a few pounds, and every pound lost is gain for the horse. Also, a well-conditioned rider helps the horse cope with weight. We normally load our pack animals with only around 150 pounds, because the load is static. But a good rider moves with the horse, leaning this way and that as necessary.

The best thing we riders can do to condition ourselves is to ride, ride, ride. But a routine of exercise and calisthenics, or a weight program, can make you a better rider. The biggest physical limitation I see among clients relates to leg strength. Lack of it makes for unbalanced riding, inability to support oneself with the stirrups, and difficulty giving leg cues. A person who is top-heavy and weak in the legs rides with less security and is also harder on the horse.

CHAPTER EIGHT

THE HUNTING HORSE

Many westerners live for the experience of hunting with horses in big mountain country. Here the author's sons David and Jonathan glass for elk at dawn, with Chief tied nearby.

Y ou may not be a hunter, and you may have absolutely no interest in becoming one, but please don't skip this chapter. I suspect you'll find things within it that apply elsewhere.

No human activity is more intertwined with horsemanship than hunting (excepting, perhaps, warfare). From the earliest domestication of the horse, humans found that equine allies made them more effective in gathering food on the hoof, and in many respects, this hasn't changed in hundreds of years. Mongolian hunters, neck-reining their spirited horses while balancing a trained golden eagle on one arm, pursue prey as large as wolves, which, incredibly, the eagles are able to kill.

Through the American South and, to a degree, on the Great Plains, bird hunters search for quail, grouse, and other edible birds on horseback, their pointing dogs quivering in place as a signal that the human hunter must dismount and move forward. The horses are fast-moving and gaited. Hunting horseback allows the hunters and dogs to cover far more ground than the hunter could handle on foot. Although I've never participated, I've had clients who have hunted sharp-tailed grouse and "prairie chickens" on the prairies of the Dakotas this way, so I've had a bit of vicarious experience. The hunters tend to look for hard-charging, ground-covering horses.

Field trials on horseback are another popular activity for which horses are traditional and required, both by the nature of the activity and by the sponsoring organizations. Here the emphasis is not on hunting itself (blanks are normally fired at the birds that flush in front of the dogs) but on the performance of the pointing dogs used. Gaited horses are used exclusively for field trials, and their riders, both contestants and judges, alternate between a fast running walk or foxtrot and a canter (lope) to keep up with dogs that can cover ten miles in a single hour.

Although this activity may seem far removed from backcountry horse use, it's really not. The country is normally open and somewhat wild, and several of the training requirements are equally useful in any remote area. The horses must tolerate gunfire and dogs, and they must be able to stand "ground tied." We'll touch on these later.

Following hounds on horseback is an activity that goes back to the Grecian Empire. The first published "natural horseman," Xenophon wrote extensive treatises on both horses and hunting dogs. The British and eastern US tradition of foxhunting, following hounds over hills and fences, is well known. Out west, Theodore Roosevelt chased wolves and coyotes with hounds, and nearly all his hunting for other species involved horses, even in Africa where before the advent of the Land Rover, horseback hunting and equine transport of safari equipment was the norm. And, of course, the Plains Indian tribes flourished when the horse became available for following and chasing the buffalo herds.

For me, though, the term "hunting horse" invokes memories of elk hunting camps in painted aspen groves, wood smoke curling from the chimney of the tent stove, and a highline with horses and mules, sweaty after a day of hard work, munching pellets from their feed bags. In the Rocky Mountain West, backcountry horse use and wilderness hunting are as intertwined today as they were in Roosevelt's time. I'd venture to say that hunting expeditions are the most common single use of the backcountry horse in the Rocky Mountains.

I tried to explain this once to an editor of a magazine for which I wrote many columns who apparently didn't approve of hunting. Many of my best photographs and most memorable experiences with trail horses had come during hunting expeditions, but she wanted them excluded, wanted only material that celebrated trail riding "purely for the joy of it." No wonder the magazine involved was rarely read by the Montana backcountry horsemen I knew; for them, the horse experience and the hunting experience were inseparable.

GUNFIRE

Certain qualities and specific training are indicated for the horse that's going to take its rider on a wilderness hunting expedition, perhaps over icy trails and difficult terrain, often off trail. Tolerance for gunfire may be the item that comes to mind, but it's probably of less concern than for the field trial or bird hunting horses that will be subjected to hundreds of rounds detonated, often close to them, in the course of a day. The big-game hunter only fires his rifle very occasionally, perhaps only once or twice on a trip, and often not at all.

An old joke among guides and outfitters in the Rockies concerns the "dude" (paying hunter) who, when introduced to the horse he'll be riding, asks, "Can I shoot off this horse?" The guide answers, "Yeah—once!" In other words, the hunter may trigger one shot, but the guide won't guarantee what will happen next, and the hunter is likely to be bucked into the dirt.

Yes, under certain circumstances, a rifle can be fired from a trained horse, and Cowboy action shooters train their animals to perform with pistols shot by their riders. But big-game rifles have a great deal of muzzle blast, and for the most part, shooting one from the back of a horse is not safe, humane, or accurate. Western movies aside, when the US Cavalry needed to cut loose with gunfire, the men normally dismounted. Every fourth man held the horses of the others, and a picket line was formed. Then the soldiers could unleash accurate fire.

I read of a cavalry procedure for gunfire training that involved loose horses in an arena with a reward station in the middle. A shot was fired, then grain was offered. This procedure was repeated, with the boldest horses coming for a reward first and the others catching on.

More recently, Cowboy mounted shooters have become the experts at training horses to withstand the report of pistols going off in rapid succession, normally ten rounds, five from each revolver. An added challenge comes from the smoke—blanks with black powder are used, the wad holding the powder in the blank cartridge being sufficient to break the balloon targets at close range.

Often a cartridge case with only a primer seated is used at the beginning for minimal noise, while the handgun itself is shown to the horse and held in various positions. Gradually the revolver is loaded with blank cartridges that make increasingly more noise, the horse gradually adjusting.

A word about any training that involves actual firearms: It's essential the human doing the training is thoroughly versed in firearms safety. A famous actor, unaware that blank cartridges expel a wad at high velocity, dangerous at close range, pointed a handgun so loaded at his head and pulled the trigger. He died.

Blank pistols, made to fire only blanks, are available at sporting outlets (they're used for starting races at track meets) and in stagecraft catalogs for use in stage plays. They are safer because they can't chamber or fire live ammunition. However, they are made to disintegrate the wad holding the powder, and that can create fragments that might sting the horse or a person standing next to you.

A trainer I once employed was adept at cracking a bullwhip. The resulting report is very similar to that of a pistol shot, and was quite effective. He'd sit on the horse softly cracking the whip off to the side, then increasing its crack as the horse became tolerant. Again, don't try this unless you're adept at cracking a bullwhip. It's more difficult than you may think, and it's easy to whip yourself, or worse, your horse.

Actually, for the first stages of firearms training a child's cap pistol works just fine and is probably the safest tool you can use. Political correctness has dimmed the popularity of these toys, but cap pistols can still be purchased. The caps explode a tiny charge of black powder, just enough to give the horse a whiff of its distinctive odor. Getting him used to progressively louder sounds is pretty much like any other "sacking out" exercise.

Whether you'll ever hunt or not, firearms training for your horse is worthwhile. You'll probably ride where a hunting season is in progress, or perhaps near a rifle range. Cars can backfire. Training to tolerate the unique sound of gunfire is a plus all around.

GROUND TYING

Of the dozens of horses Theodore Roosevelt owned and loved during his lifetime, a gelding named Manitou stands out, particularly within Roosevelt's experience in the West. Named after an Algonquian mythological figure with special spiritual power, Manitou lived up to his name multiple times. When a group of young Sioux braves charged toward Roosevelt at full gallop, Manitou held his ground, enabling his rider to do so as well. A dicey situation was defused.

Then there was the time the somewhat impetuous young Roosevelt decided to cross the Little Missouri, which was running high with spring runoff and was full of ice chunks from the annual breakup. Both horse and man nearly drowned, more than once disappearing under the chocolate colored water. While he dried himself out in front of a woodstove, TR told a horrified friend and witness that he never would have attempted the crossing were he with any other horse than Manitou. The horse with the spirit name was like a big brother to Roosevelt— or maybe a guardian angel.

Among the gelding's many attributes was his habit of staying put, untied, even without hobbles, grazing on a patch of grass while Roosevelt stalked game, sometimes for hours at a time. No, he wasn't ground tied. He simply seems to have understood that he was to stay within a few yards of where he was left until his master returned. This is all the more remarkable when we recall the sort of country involved—big and open, with no fences to stop a drifting horse.

Few if any of us will ever own a horse we could rely upon to graze in a small area for hours, untied, and be there upon our return. But we can appreciate the value of a horse trained to ground tie. Frankly, I've never spent the time on this with my own trainees that I probably should have, no doubt because of my western orientation. One of the most fundamental principles of horsemanship in the Big Open is holding on to your horse. Without him, traditionally and even today, one's very survival could be in jeopardy.

But for short periods of time, when a needed task while you're dismounted requires two hands and there's nowhere to tie up, a horse trained to stand in place is incredibly useful. Methods for getting him trained to ground tie are all over the map in variety. Years ago I read of a man who trained to ground tie by carrying a weight which he could snap onto a rein when he dismounted. Then he'd command the horse to "whoa." Already well trained to yield to the bit, the horse, feeling a bit of pressure from the weight when he moved, would stay put, especially with his trainer nearby, repeating whoa as needed.

Another method involved strategically placed stakes driven deeply into the ground, unobtrusive in tall grass. A ring was attached to each stake. With a snap on lead rope or rein, the trainer could get off, snap to the ring, say, "Whoa," then move away. The horse would assume it was the ground itself tying him, and stay put.

A website from the field trial world describes the use of an "E-collar," an electronic collar capable of producing a mild shock, for training to ground tie. Yes, these collars exist for horses, and they're not to be confused with those for dogs—horses are more sensitive to shock and the collars used are much milder. My reaction when I first heard of them was similar to that of a friend and trainer who exclaimed, "Those things are going to cause a lot of wrecks and ruin a lot of horses."

I suspect a proponent would counter by saying that as with any training device, a longe whip or a long lead rope, such collars are merely extensions of one's arm, that if used very carefully they're no less humane. I have heard they've been used successfully on extremely aggressive horses, the type that will corner another animal and inflict serious injury.

I've never used an equine E-collar, and I'm not tempted to ever do so. But I've used the canine type on my Brittany spaniels and Airedales, and in our location they've been lifesavers. Our ranch house is next to a busy two-lane highway that has claimed the lives of too many cats and dogs in the past decades. An absolute "No!" is a survival requirement—I must be able to stop the dog in his tracks if he heads toward the traffic. Before the E-collar is ever introduced the dogs have been trained to the limits and requirements of the regular collar and its check cord, however—that's required. For a succinct argument in favor of E-collars for horses you might consider perusing horsemanship practitioner Clinton Anderson's writing on the subject. He points out the advantage that the horse doesn't know you are the one administering the correction. The horse believes it's his action that causes the stimulation.

Anderson's argument reminds me of my father-in-law's elbow. Elmer was very skillful at placing a quick poke with his elbow into the chest of an overzealous horse, and he was sneaky about it—the horse was unaware that the poke came from Elmer. "I don't want him to be mad at me," Elmer said. "I want him to be mad at himself for doing what caused the poke, so he won't do it again."

Since E-collars have become standard equipment for most trainers of hunting dogs, it's not surprising the equine version would gain acceptance in that world. For ground tie training, the method I've seen described involves tying something benign to the lead rope, such as a clump of knots in a rope. This clump lies on the ground. The trainer, working with a horse already accustomed to the collar, reinforces "Whoa" with a slight electric stimulation whenever the horse pulled on the rope enough to make the clump of knots move on the ground.

All these methods for teaching ground tying involve some sort of physical restraint, but you can teach ground tying by simple patience, by using the same approach you use with any round-pen training. Whether you favor the longe whip or the long lead rope, you've probably taught your horse these things: impulsion, changing direction by turning around facing you, and "whoa." Once he's well-versed in those, teaching to ground tie becomes an extension of the "whoa" command which, with horses as in hunting dogs, means not only "stop" but "stay." Dropping the lead rope to the ground takes on a particular meaning when accompanied by the command. Take your time, be persistent, and you'll get it done.

Would I trust ground tying on a true wilderness expedition, when I had to leave a horse in place to stalk an elk or set up a camp? No. Potential is too great for loss of the horse, injury to it, or putting myself afoot in remote country. I wouldn't expect ground tie training to overcome the fright caused by a bear passing nearby, a sudden hailstorm, or any other eventuality for which it would be very hard to train. But having a horse that will stand without moving for a short time while you accomplish a task requiring both hands is an asset indeed.

HANDLING THE GEAR AND THE GAME

In the last chapter we discussed handling weight on horses, on keeping it forward close to the horse's center of gravity, and why riding with a backpack is anathema, horrible both for the horse and for your safety. The problem with hunting and horses is that the nature of the activity tends to add even more weight and bulk to the horse's challenge. One of the more awkward items needed is the rifle or shotgun. The shotgun is an easier proposition, because it's normally slick, light, and lacking a scope.

Rifles today have tended to gain weight and bulk because of technology. Oversized scopes with protruding knobs, bipods, and other accessories aren't very scabbard-friendly. The problem is usually handled these days by large, padded, synthetic scabbards that fully enclose the rifle. Another way

A fully enclosed scabbard protected my rifle from severe weather on this hunt with my trusty gelding Partner.

to handle the issue is to eschew these developments, sticking with more compact, traditional firearms—but that's another story.

The scabbard can be carried on either side of the horse. I prefer that the rifle ride butt forward, muzzle down, at about a 45-degree angle. The scabbard lies under the stirrup leather, and dropping the muzzle tends to reduce the size of the lump, moving it down toward your calf instead of riding directly under your knee.

Accustoming Chief to the scabbard and rifle.

Too many rifle scabbards come with inadequate straps that are weak and too short to make for easy attachment. Add better and longer straps if necessary, and do this fitting at home, not at the trailhead in the dark. I like to run the front strap up through the gullet of the saddle and the rear strap up to a D-ring on the side of the cantle. If your saddle lacks a D-ring, the rear strap must be secured to saddle strings. Better yet, take your backcountry saddle to a good saddle maker and ask him to add D-rings behind the cantle, low on each side, and one in the middle for attaching a crupper. While he's at it, ask for two more, one on each side of the pommel. You'll find so many uses for them you'll wonder why most saddles are made without them.

Start carrying a rifle horseback (always empty, without a round in the chamber) well before that dark morning at the trailhead when you're off on a hunt. Otherwise you may be in for an unpleasant surprise. Lining the rifle up for insertion into the scabbard puts it near the horse's eye. Practice inserting and withdrawing the rifle, remembering that under hunting conditions you may be withdrawing it quickly and clumsily while everyone, horses and companions alike, are excited at spotting an elk herd.

Practice carrying rifle and gear well before the hunt. Chief was a little concerned with the pressure caused by the scabbard.

You've trained your horse to respond to leg cues. Now, particularly if the rifle scabbard is on the left side, your horse gets a giant unaccustomed leg cue when your foot puts pressure on the stirrup that pushes the scabbard against his body. With a few sessions you'll get him used to it, but if he's the thin-skinned type he may want to move forward when he feels that extra "cue" the first time.

Even light rifles put some weight on one side of the saddle. Compensate by hanging your binoculars and canteen off the horn on the opposite side. If necessary, load your saddlebags with one side heavier as a counterweight to the rifle. Riding all day when the saddle continually tries to rotate to one side is no fun, and it's difficult for the horse as well.

The saddle scabbard isn't likely to be the only new experience for your horse, at least if you are lucky enough to secure your winter's meat supply. Some horses are terrified by the smell of downed deer or the blood and entrails that are removed during field dressing. However, this isn't a given. Perhaps I've been fortunate, but none of my horses or mules thus far have seemed particularly afraid.

An old-timers' trick is to place blood from the downed animal on the horse's nose, the idea, I suppose, a version of the "flooding therapy" mentioned earlier. I've never seen the need to do this, but I wouldn't rule it out. It's just as likely the animal is afraid of the sight of game on the ground. Years ago, lucky enough to draw a rare moose permit in Montana, I was able to harvest a young bull that proved to be such good meat that our family practically cried when the last package disappeared from the freezer.

I had skinned the animal in place, and it turned out that one of my horses was fixated on the hide of the animal. He was so intent on it that he scarcely noticed my struggles to place a hind quarter in each of his saddle panniers. Those he carried back to camp as unconcerned as he'd been while carrying supplies.

A few years ago, while writing my book on Theodore Roosevelt's hunting experiences as compared to my own, I tried to capture the essence of TR's Great Plains forays for antelope. Emily and I hunted them horseback, a rifle in a vintage caliber riding in my saddle scabbard. When I found and put down a young pronghorn buck I had no idea how Partner, my young gelding, would react. To my surprise he and Emily's horse Scooter were totally unconcerned, grazing close to the downed animal as if an antelope buck lying on the ground was an everyday sight.

When I hefted the buck onto Partner's saddle, the spirited young gelding stood like a rock. His only spook came when one of the animal's legs, not well secured by my tie efforts, came loose and projected out into the horse's peripheral vision. That caused a quick unscheduled lunging through several circles—but that was all. I led the horse back to the road to a point where the buck could be retrieved by vehicle, dropped the animal off my saddle, and rode back to camp.

Partner, though only a colt, carried the pronghorn with very little drama.

There may be times when it's possible to drag a deer or elk back to camp or your vehicle, particularly if there's snow on the ground. Snow makes the critter slide more easily, and it also pads the meat from bruising. Whether or not you ever intend to drag game, teaching your horse to drag loads from the saddle horn can be useful in many ways. You can drag a firewood log back to camp and "motivate" a recalcitrant pack animal with a pull from the saddle horn if your horse understands how to lean into the load. In an emergency, you might be able to pull a floundering horse out of a bog.

The competitive roping horse is trained to face the roped calf and maintain a steady pressure, keeping the slack out of the rope while its rider dismounts and ties the animal. For backcountry purposes, we'll emphasize handling pressure the opposite way, pulling while walking away from the load. To prepare your horse make sure he's completely comfortable with a rope sliding all over his body. Toss it over the saddle, over his rump, pull it around, and rub it on him.

Then, while riding, carry a soft rope perhaps twenty feet long and casually drop it over his side to the ground while at a walk. Your horse may walk a little sideways as he eyeballs the rope sliding like a snake to his rear, but just be patient and you'll get him over that. Drag the empty rope behind you, first on one side, then the other. At this point simply holding it in one hand is safest for both you and your horse. A dally around the horn isn't yet needed, and you must never wrap it around your hand.

When your horse is thoroughly at ease with dragging an empty rope, attach a light weight. A small tire provides a fair amount of resistance, yet is relatively quiet. To handle the pressure on the rope you may have to take a "dally," meaning a wrap or two around the horn, always with your thumb in the air. The horse will feel considerable resistance, even dragging a small tire, and he'll now experience a bit of noise caused by the object he's dragging. Train him to drag it on each side, then to turn and face it while you pass the slackened rope over his head and turn around.

Travis drags a light tire, a good beginning load, with Scooter.

If your saddle horn is relatively slippery, cut a cross section about an inch wide from a piece of inner tube. Wrap this circular strip of rubber by encircling the horn, twisting and putting the loop back over the horn, twisting again, and so on. You'll coat the horn with an easily removable layer of rubber that helps hold the dally against pressure, probably allowing you to take just one wrap for quick and safe removal of the rope should something go wrong.

For pulling any substantial load you'll want to use a breast collar. The type I like is sometimes called a "pulling collar," because it fits at the base of the horse's neck where it joins the shoulders, not horizontally across the front of the chest. The pulling collar works on the same principle as draft horse collar seen on a harness designed for heavy work. It's easier on the horse than the breast-strap type, doesn't interfere with his breathing, and it allows substantial loads to be dragged. Historically, the horse collar on harnesses is counted as a major development in civilization, because it substantially multiplied the loads draft animals could pull. Pulling an object from the saddle horn, of course, is less efficient than the draft horse's traces, which are placed much lower, because the point of attachment to the horse is so high. Pulling from the horn provides less leverage.

Still, impressive loads can be moved. During late-season elk hunts in the Gardiner, Montana, area before the northern elk herd was shrunk to one fourth its size by introduced wolves, many families filled their freezers with the excellent meat of a cow elk. These late hunts, intended to control overpopulation of the Yellowstone herd, were held in early winter, and there was usually plenty of snow. Retrieval was by horse, often on trails through the snow that became iced up like bobsled runs when used over and over.

These late hunts could involve some adventure. On one of them I'd shot a big cow elk and field dressed it in very deep snow. The initial pull of a mile or so was tough for my big gelding Rockytop, but when we hit a track on a road, things got better. Until, that is, I looked ahead to find a herd of bison straddling the road. This was an eventuality Rockytop's training had not included, but there was no turning back. The big gelding eyeballed the herd, then like a trooper, lowered his head to the pull and forged forward. The bison split to allow us through, stared, but showed no hostile intent. Still, I breathed more easily on the other side of the herd.

Partner equipped with a pulling collar as David heads for the backcountry. The rein chains are also of interest—they add a slight collection and also protect the leather rein sections from immersion when the horse drinks.

We then hit one of those iced-over trails, and the pull became so much easier that Rockytop picked up the pace to a nice flat walk. We headed down a slight grade to the campground, chock-full of hunters with their campers and tents, and the game wardens that so closely monitored these late hunts. The entire surface of the camping area was glare ice, but Rockytop was sharp-shod, and the ice didn't seem to bother him in the least. So I let him pick up to a running walk that he maintained right through the campground to my horse trailer, Rockytop looking as if he were intent on winning a show class, yet pulling a five-hundred-pound cow elk.

All eyes stared at us; talking suspended. The hunters were a more gratifying audience than any I ever experienced in the grandstands of a horse show, and the experience was punctuated by the question of an outfitter who had watched us intently with a smile on his face. "What kind of a horse is that?" he asked.

"He's a ranch-raised Tennessee Walking Horse," I replied, dropping the drag rope.

As I tied Rockytop to the horse trailer the outfitter said, "Lookin' good."

CHAPTER NINE

LONG EARS AND SHORT TAILS: A MULE PRIMER

The scene is crystal clear and brilliantly colored, though it's been in my mind for well over half a century. I sit on a rock with my companions, a rancher and his son and my father. To our right, several hundred feet below us, is a lake, shimmering, emerald. A hundred feet above us on a rock face, the ledge trail we've just traversed, comes a single rider, felt cowboy hat cocked to one side, his slim body in the loose slouch of a man who spends much of his life in the saddle. He moves with the horse as if the two are one.

But it's what follows the man and his bay horse that command most of my boyhood attention. He's leading a string of mules, all neatly packed. They walk with the same easy grace the man exhibits in the saddle. Where are they going? What sort of camp will they share, and how long will they stay?

We had backpacked to a high mountain lake which at that time allowed semipermanent camps on its shores along with boats equipped with outboard motors for trolling. The rancher owned such a camp consisting of a large, framed, wall tent and a boat whose motor was stored in a locker made from a fifty-five-gallon drum. He and his son had invited my father and me to accompany them on a trip of several nights to stay in the camp across the lake and catch a "mess" of fish.

I remember many details of the camp—angleworms for bait that froze during the night, then came to life when left in the sun; the rancher's pancakes; trout dinners from the icy lake, fried in a cast-iron pan after being rolled in cornmeal. But it's that line of mules and the packer who led them that created the most indelible picture.

I knew a little about mules. I'd listened to the stories of men who packed into the backcountry, and Sigurd, our host rancher, had used two draft mules to pull a wagon in the local parade. I suppose I held mules in a sort of awe, mingled respect and fear. But all those I'd seen were packed or harnessed. During my boyhood I'm not sure I ever saw a mule being ridden.

Go to the same backcountry today and you'll see even more mules than I did as a boy, many packed with panniers and manties, but also a good number carrying riders. Interest in mules seems to have skyrocketed since then. Today there are mule clinicians, many books on mules, and television programs that feature training tips for mule owners. Long ears are now fashionable, and I'd advise caution to anyone who treats a mule rider as if he's riding an inferior equine. Do so and you're likely to get an unpleasant response.

Saddle mules have become extremely popular. (Billy Oley up.)

And yet, in spite of the interest, we're amazed at the number of fairly experienced horsemen who visit our ranch and show confusion when dealing with the subject of mules and donkeys. Some refer to mules as donkeys or donkeys as mules. Others ask about mule reproduction, and many repeat old and tired (and not very accurate) stereotypes about mule behavior.

So when talking about mules, it's best to start from the beginning. A mule is the sterile hybrid offspring of a donkey sire (called a jack) and a female horse (a mare). Yes, it can work the other way, too, offspring from a male horse (stallion) and a female donkey (jenny). The result of that less common breeding produces a hinny, normally considered less useful than a mule.

Why sterile? Horses have sixty-four chromosomes, donkeys just sixty-two, and the resulting offspring (mules) have sixty-three, which doesn't work for reproduction. Indeed, according to a story in the *Denver Post*, the Romans had the saying *cum mula peperit*, meaning "when a mule foals," which they used as an equivalent of "when hell freezes over."

But hold on. You've probably read of several scientifically verified cases of a molly mule giving birth. It has happened. But its odds are akin to yours of winning the Powerball jackpot, so the statement that mules are sterile continues to be pretty accurate.

That said, molly mules do have reproductive cycles, though they're usually muted and often scarcely noticeable. And male mules (johns) must be gelded (castrated) or they'll become real monsters.

With that out of the way, what's so special about mules? First, they're the ultimate in hybrid vigor, because their parents are so dissimilar. The horse and the donkey are not just separate "breeds"; they're separate species. Hybrid vigor tends to be associated with long life, superior resistance to disease, and a special, though hard to define, physical strength. Mules have all of these.

The first prominent American to recognize these qualities was none other than George Washington, who along with being the father of our country was the father of mule breeding in the US. First given a breeding jack by the king of Spain, then a second one later on, Washington talked mules with anyone who would listen, even at cabinet meetings. He was convinced that the hot, humid South could not be successfully farmed without them, and he was probably right. His jacks went on breeding tours, and he kept records of their progeny.

In Spain Emily and I saw some beautiful mules nearly everywhere in the southern mountains. Some mules were packing loads, others carrying cattlemen checking their herds, and still others ran loose, retirees, it was explained, once owned by farmers who couldn't part with them, and now simply kept on as pets. At a busy intersection in one small city we watched a loose mule stop at a red light, then proceed along with traffic when the light turned.

When we commented on the attractiveness of the mules we saw, our guide gave us the reason. In Spain, she said, you breed only your very best mare to get a mule. Mules are special, revered. You stack the odds of getting a good one in your favor by choosing a proven jack and your best mare.

A fine-looking young mule, sired by a jack and a Tennessee Walking Horse mare.

Unfortunately, the same cannot be said for some mule breeding in the US. Too often someone consigns his or her worst mare to the job of breeding a mule. I still hear it too often. Someone owns a mare that's deficient in one way or another, so the owner says, "I'd just as well try to get a mule out of her."

My usual reply is to quote our guide in Spain and say, "Why don't you pick out the real jewel from your herd, the mare that everyone wants to ride, and breed her to the jack instead?"

Haphazard and ill-advised breeding may be responsible for some of the negative stereotypes of mules. We hear them all the time—stubborn, inclined to kick, and so on—and there certainly is a germ of truth in some of them. But the reasons may not be as a true hater of mules, the local-color humorist "Josh Billings" (Henry Wheeler Shaw) proclaimed in his essay "Essa on the Muel." This essay was the first in which he adopted colloquial spelling and dialect, and the piece was a hit.

Some gems from the piece:

> The mule is haf hoss and haf Jackass, and then kums to a full stop, natur diskovering her mistake.

And,

> You kan trust them with e n n y one whose life aint worth enny more than the mules. The only wa tu keep the mules into a paster, is tu turn them in- o a medder jineing, and let them jump out.

Well, it's true that mules are sterile, but probably not because nature discovered her mistake. And it's true also that mules can jump, often from a standing position. As to trustworthiness, there's even something to that, because when a mule kicks, it kicks. A government study was once done to determine why a mule's kick was more likely to be fatal than that of a horse. It turned out to be a matter of velocity—the hoof traveled faster than that from a horse's kick—and mules can also "cow kick," meaning that they can kick forward and out to the side.

If these things have some truth, why is it that mule riders are so fiercely loyal to the animals? Talk to a confirmed mule addict and he or she is likely to imply that once the mule experience starts, you'll never go back to a horse. To hear some of them tell it horses are unsafe, unpredictable, and so helpless in rough country that they're likely to fall off the trail.

Why is it also that professional packers almost always prefer mules for their strings, though they may lead the string with a saddle horse? Ask one and he's likely to say, "Well, when you get good ones and they get used to their work you just don't have to mess with them. They just do their thing without any fuss." Certainly the Grand Canyon mules are testimony to the accuracy of the packers' preference. Through more than a century of travel to the bottom of the canyon hauling inexperienced tourists, there hasn't been a single accident.

There's no doubt that mules have many advantages as backcountry animals both under saddle and pack. Horses are descended from open-country animals, donkeys from rocky, mountainous regions. Mules inherit many of their best traits from the donkey side of the equation including smaller, tougher feet and uncanny surefootedness. Donkeys have another trait as well, some of which the mule inherits. They tend to be less spooky than a horse. An unexpected eventuality will often cause the donkey to do one of three things, study, spook, or attack. The horse's first impulse is almost always to flee. The mule inherits some of the donkey's coolness under pressure.

Certainly mules can spook, but they have another trait that tends to prevent blind, irrational explosions, a trait that also causes accusations of stubbornness. This is their highly developed sense of self-preservation. They don't like risk. This trait is to your benefit on a ledge trail, but it also caused mules to be useless in battle. They are simply too smart to wantonly get themselves shot. They've done yeoman's service as pack and draft animals supporting armies during many wars, including recently in the Middle East, but they don't care to lead a charge into enemy fire.

Mules also tend to be comfortable to ride, even if they aren't gaited. A mule from a nongaited dam usually has a smoother trot than her mother. I've carefully watched such mules trot, and I believe some of them break the two beats of the trot very slightly. I'd haven't been able to slow video down to verify this, but I've noted it with donkeys as well, and even a split-second difference in the impact of the two opposing feet (i.e., left front and right rear), so slight as not to be readily noticeable or heard, can reduce the impact.

But mules are also comfortable because of their builds. Their bodies are invariably narrower than those of their mothers, and with mules as well as with horses, that trait makes for a more comfortable day in the saddle. Straddling a barrel-bellied horse is not only hard on your hips, it's also terribly tough for your knees, because they're being asked to bend two ways. They're not designed to do that!

And if those weren't advantages enough for the saddle mule, most from nongaited mares can outwalk their mothers. Mules are often fast walkers, and few have the problem discussed earlier of tending to pick up to a trot or jog at a slow speed. And, of course, if the dam is gaited, the walk tends to be better yet.

But one caveat where a mule's build is concerned: few of them have the good withers of the sort of saddle horse I prefer. Also, their backs tend to be straighter, lacking the natural saddle build of many horses. Because of this trait, a crupper or breeching is normally required to keep the saddle from sliding forward on downhill grades.

Mules are definitely more intelligent than horses, and a recent British study suggests they're more intelligent than donkeys as well. A mule likes to think things over. *Can I do this? Will it hurt me?* And a horseman who expects immediate and unquestioning obedience from his horse is likely to chalk this tendency up to stubbornness.

But one must not get carried away by these differences. Most of the training techniques you've learned for horses work for mules as well. My impression is that you need to be more careful, take your time, and at all costs, hold your temper. It may seem at first that a mule is slower to learn, but I suspect it's because he spends more time in that "thinking" stage, figuring out what might happen to him. A favorite saying is that a mule demands the sort of training every horse should have.

We had packed into the wilderness north of Yellowstone Park, grizzly country, an area slowly recovering the beauty that was marred but far from extinguished by the devastation of massive fires twenty years earlier. We were looking for elk while knowing that chances were extremely slim. The northern Yellowstone elk herd had been decimated by new neighbors, large northern Canadian wolves introduced several years earlier. The moose were completely gone, the elk herd reduced to one fifth its earlier size, but we went to the wilderness for the best reason—we simply had to go.

There were just two of us, my friend and physician Billy and me, and five good Tennessee Walking Horses: my old reliable cow horse Little Mack, a tall black gelding named Skywalker, Emily's do-everything gelding Redstar, and Billy's two grays, Smokey and Blaze. We made camp in a green little valley that had largely escaped the fires, rigged a highline for the horses and the tent for us, had a good supper, and, since the daylight still lingers long in September, prepared for a pleasant evening by a campfire.

Everything worked that way until the last step—a drizzle set in just after supper and soon became a light but steady rain. We were up there for the elbow room wilderness provides and were not about to spend the evening within the confines of the tent. Instead, we rigged a tarp overhead, managed to build a small but smoky fire, put a lantern on a makeshift table, and spent a couple of hours visiting about wilderness, horses, and, after a couple of bourbon-laced Cokes, mules.

Mules had been front and center in our discussion with a friend and retired outfitter who knew this wilderness intimately. He spent his entire career in this area guiding hunters and fishermen and taking his own family to a special area off-trail, whose location he was kind enough to share with us. The route to this special place was tough, very tough, and Billy and I had decided not to attempt it. But in describing the area, the outfitter had said, "I know you have good horses, but do you have any mules?"

When the chips were down, this man trusted mules more than any horses, including his own. He believed in that edge, maybe slight when compared to the best horses, that mules have in sure-footedness, ability to negotiate deadfall and bogs, and he was hoping that we'd be able to choose mules should we attempt travel to the place he described. And Billy and I, discussing this later, found ourselves wanting to do something about the situation.

Neither of us had ever found our horses wanting in any respect. I'd crossed the highest, toughest passes in the mountains of southern Montana on Little Mack, and earlier I'd traveled solo from Yellowstone Park over two mountain passes to a trailhead near my home, and I'd done it on Major, a big, strong gelding, when he was only three, my light packs carried by another three-year-old. No, our horses had been outstanding.

But something else was factoring in. We'd been hearing about the substantial prices being commanded by saddle mules. Add "gaited" to the description, and the prices edged even higher. Wouldn't it make sense to acquire a gaited jack to breed to some of our Tennessee Walking horse mares, and get some mules for our own use while also cashing in on this trend? So, at some point under the tarp and the steady rain, I blurted out, "Billy, we ought to go in together and buy a gaited jack!"

"Let's do it," he said, enthusiastically. And that high-altitude decision was the reason "Bubba the Gaited Jack," registered as "Bud" in the stud book of the American Gaited Mule Association, came to Montana. He arrived from the farm of the late Bill Moore, a guru in the world of gaited

Bubba the Gaited Jack was quickly started under saddle by Travis Young.

mules. Just two and a half years old, he stepped out of a transport trailer on a December day, felt the chill, watched the drifting snowflakes, and darted into the barn.

Bubba proved gentle and easy to train. Travis quickly got him under saddle. Though he trotted occasionally, he was definitely gaited, varying his way of going through amble, foxtrot, and flat walk, all of them looking easy and natural. But as a breeder he was reluctant—the mares scared him, and he scared them. However, we were equipped to collect semen and artificially inseminate—we had shipped semen from one of our stallions for many years—and we received help from another source, a gentle jenny we named Bubbette. We built a simple "phantom" for Bubba to mount, and Bubbette, standing behind a panel in front, was inducement enough.

Emily imprints one of our first mule foals.

The spring following Bubba's first year in Montana featured something new for us. Our field full of broodmares sported spirited little creatures with long ears, mule foals whose mothers did not seem to notice anything new or different and attended them as well as they had the offspring of our stallions.

In the world of mule skinners, I consider myself an amateur. Mules came to me relatively late in life, and too few have passed through my corrals to allow anything other than broad generalizations. The hybrid vigor is a given, though, of course, all healthy foals are lively. We do watch the mule foals a bit more closely at weaning time, not because of meanness, but simply because of their physical attributes. Running and playing they'll spontaneously "cow-kick" off to the side, not aiming at anything, just "kicking up their heels." But you don't want to be in the way.

I believe it's true that mules mature more slowly than other equines, and it's said they live on average five to ten years longer than horses. That suggests that training can come a bit later as well. Many mule folks believe a mule should be around seven years old before it's really ready to use. However, it's hard to generalize. Bessie, a sorrel molly out of a Tennessee Walking Horse/Belgian cross mare, proved so tractable from the very beginning that we didn't hesitate to pack her into hunting camp this fall at age two and a half. Because of her youth, we did not load her heavily, but she handled her packs with easy grace and proved to be one of the best equine citizens in camp.

We've noticed that mules carrying packs seem to pick up some things more quickly than most horses. For instance, they quickly learn to give trees along the trail a bit wider berth, banging them into the bark less frequently. Avoiding the scraping, the noise, and the resistance that can require breaking gait makes the task easier for the mule, and they quickly figure that out.

Am I ready to sell my horses and join the growing ranks of those who insist that mules are better for everything, all the time, than horses? No. The thrill I get riding a spirited, beautiful horse, one like Chief, my young gray gelding who arches his neck and hits a six-miles-per-hour flat walk with the merest release of an ounce of rein, is not an experience I'll let go. But I respect mules and am gathering a few special ones for myself. And I suspect all future mountain trips will include some of these long-eared hybrids and the mountain music of their braying.

CHAPTER 10

PACKING UP
FOR THE TRAIL

To a novice of the sort I was as a young boy, watching the packer described in the last chapter, the whole business of putting a load on a horse or mule so that it will stay there over hill and dale may seem something akin to alchemy or voodoo. Packing is both science and art, and it's understandable that anyone inexperienced could find it intimidating, especially if he or she hears talk of such mysteries as diamond hitches, manties, and pigtails.

But there's another way of looking at it. Since learning "on the job" is best, especially if you're lucky enough to find some experienced instruction, don't hesitate to plunge right in. Learn a little at a time. I've read that the best way to become a competent mushroom hunter is to learn one safe species, and really learn it, so you're absolutely sure of that one safe mushroom and there's no way you can mistake it for another. Then, eventually, learn another, and then a third, and so on.

I live near a fine trout stream. Back when I could find more time to fish, I'd go down to the stream relatively frequently and fish with a spinning reel and lures. The limit was generous and the fish were tasty. Usually within an hour I'd catch four or five trout, enough for supper for our growing family. I was tempted to try fly fishing. It looked like fun, and I'd heard that it was. But experts in the activity talked of tying flies to "match the hatch," and named types of flies and other pieces of equipment with terminology that was Greek to me.

One summer our Marine Reserve unit was designated to serve as mountain warfare instructors in the High Sierra of California. I watched a couple of my fellow officers fly fish for golden trout in a small stream that ran near our base camp. What they were doing did not look difficult, but I expressed my reservations to one of the lieutenants. "Oh, just do it," he said. "I'll give you a couple of basic flies and tell you a few things to pick up. No need to spend much money." And, he repeated, "Just do it."

Upon return I followed the lieutenant's advice, picked up a new, inexpensive fly rod and reel, and headed down to the stream. And, in about an hour, I'd caught four or five trout for supper. I enjoyed myself and wondered why I'd waited so long to try this new variation on an exciting activity. I'd been intimidated for no good reason, and packing can offer the same obstacle.

There's no feeling quite like packing up your animals with everything you need to make a comfortable camp in the wilderness. In our highly mechanized world there's something about the self-sufficiency of the activity, the independence of it, that appeals to our souls. Become a packer and you'll find that when you return from a trip, tired, perhaps sore, craving hot showers and the amenities of home, you will, within just a day or two, find yourself planning the next trip.

So, follow the advice I was given and "just do it." Start small, hopefully with some hands-on instruction. Many clinics are sponsored by Backcountry

Backcountry horseman and trainer Logan Gehlhausen.

Horseman of American. My own clinic and that of my friend Logan Gehl-hausen prove useful to many. But even if you're on your own, with some reading, practice, and gentle animals, you can soon be hitting the trail.

But there are really two parts to this. Training your horse and teaching techniques to yourself go hand in hand. Let's start with the horse. And let's reflect that to be a part of the pack string, he needs to learn two different roles. To make him a complete backcountry animal he should both learn to be packed and learn to pony pack animals up the trail. That makes him a very versatile animal.

Carrying a packsaddle and its loads should not be difficult for the trained saddle horse, though surprises are always possible. The two major areas of concern are the breeching (often called "britchin') under the tail and the nature of the loads. If you've already trained your saddle horse to be used to the crupper, a breeching shouldn't present much of a challenge. But work from the side, keeping the breeching relatively loose, so you can lift his tail out and over the horizontal strap without struggle. Then, when the breeching is in place, tug at it alternating from both sides of the horse. Horses don't like surprises, so don't be sneaky about gear that may surprise the horse later. Make sure they know it's in position and know how it will feel when things start moving around.

The saddle horse is already used to weight on his back, but weight of a rider feels and sounds different than that of packs. We especially try to minimize sound while packing our kitchen panniers by using paper towels around some items to dull sound, but things do slip and begin to clatter or ring occasionally. A good pack animal will learn to ignore the strange sounds emanating from a pack containing pots and pans and canned goods.

ENTRY LEVEL: SADDLE PANNIERS

But before we can load up our horse, we need to touch on the various systems. The very simplest, requiring little more than an extra riding saddle, are saddle panniers, two soft bags joined by a web of material with holes to fit over the horn and pommel in front, and cantle in back. The term "pannier," incidentally, is very old, of French origin but used in English by Shakespeare in *King Henry IV, Part 1.* Some saddle panniers have lids, while some are

Saddle panniers.

open. Straps are included to secure the panniers together tightly under the horse's belly.

Think of saddle panniers as an expedient, something okay for very occasional use, but a stepping-stone on your way to acquiring better gear. They certainly have their uses. Some elk hunters roll up a set of saddle panniers and tie them on behind their riding saddles. Should they harvest an elk or deer they can put the saddle panniers in place, load them with elk or deer quarters, and lead their horse back to camp.

But there are drawbacks. Since the panniers are joined at the top it's very hard to put them in place already loaded unless you have a strong partner. Otherwise, you must load them once they're fixed on the animal's back, which is more annoying for the horse and harder work for you. Balance, so critical in all packing, is more difficult to estimate—you can't weigh each side very easily.

The problem grows worse when you try to unload saddle panniers, since you can't detach each side individually. If the cargo consists of many smaller items you can unload them while they're still in place on the horse, alternating from side to side so the horse never has a full pannier across from an empty one. But if you've placed something really heavy in the saddle panniers, such as a camp woodstove, you may find it nearly impossible to lift the item up and out, especially if the horse is tall.

On a solo moose hunt I was able to place front quarters of a young moose in a set of saddle panniers while Sugar, a favorite sorrel gelding, stood patiently. (I was stronger in those days!) But there was no way I could lift them back out when I'd returned to camp. Standing on my tiptoes and reaching down into the pannier to get a good hold on the moose quarter, then lifting the hundred pounds up and out, was too much. Luckily Sugar tolerated the alternative: I made sure breast collar, breeching, and cinches on the sawbuck saddle were completely detached. Then I rolled the whole works, saddle, panniers, and quarters off Sugar's back.

There are other difficulties with this system. Unless the two sides are perfectly balanced, the panniers tend to slide off to one side or the other because the openings for the pommel and cantle are too large and sloppy to hold the panniers in place. Using them with a packsaddle tends to create the same problem. We've installed grommets centered on the front and back of the web connecting the two sides. Running a piece of rope through these, then to the saddle horn in front and the D-ring centered in the skirts behind the cantles of our saddles and tying each tightly helps prevent slipping to one side. When we've used saddle panniers on a Decker packsaddle we've added a basket hitch to each side to help stabilize the load—but that's not too practical with most riding saddles.

Another problem is lack of a breeching on most riding saddles. If you ride with a crupper, then you're better off, but without either breeching or crupper a pack load tends to slide forward on a horse equipped only with saddle panniers. This points to the main difference between human cargo and packed cargo. A good rider helps the horse. On a downhill grade he or she gains support from the stirrups. Packed loads are deadweight, and that's the reason we like to hold the total load on our pack animals to around 150 pounds. Of course, a light synthetic breeching could be brought along, or simply put in place on your saddle horse if you anticipated using the saddle panniers. And if you're riding a mule, you'll have one with you anyway.

Saddle panniers have their uses, and in this case the orange ones on the rear mule were large enough to accommodate the woodstove. Here they're carried on a sawbuck packsaddle. Slow down when leading pack animals over a stream or obstacle.

Still, saddle panniers will get you in the game if you have an extra riding saddle around. The cost is modest. Just remember to pack them evenly, and don't forget the all-important belly straps. Snug them up to keep the packs from flapping.

BETTER—SAWBUCK AND PANNIERS

The sawbuck (sometimes called the crossbuck) is an ancient packsaddle that gets its name from what used to be a common backyard appliance, a setup of crossed poles on which firewood logs were placed for cutting into blocks before splitting. Variations of the sawbuck exist throughout the world. Emily and I saw them while riding in Spain.

The saddle is really quite simple. Two sets of strong wooden slats cross, each making an X, and are attached to two "bars" of wood, fitting front to back on each side. The wooden bars are usually contoured to better fit the animal's back, and they bear just to the sides of its spine. Normally an oversized pack pad, extending farther down on each side of the animal than a regular saddle pad, fits under the sawbuck saddle. The sawbuck usually sports two web cinches, a breast strap, and a breeching.

Sawbuck saddles are versatile, light, strong, and inexpensive. As a beginning packer, you can't go wrong by purchasing a sawbuck and a set of panniers to go with it. Panniers come in many varieties, but I'd recommend soft cloth ones, either canvas reinforced on the corners with leather or a strong nylon synthetic cloth. On top such panniers normally have a wooden dowel or aluminum rod sewn into the fabric. These take the stress of the straps used to attach the panniers to the saddle, helping to hold the shape of the load.

Mule with sawbuck.

Mare being ponied with a sawbuck packsaddle on a training ride.

   Cloth panniers are relatively easy to pack. Keep softer items next to the horse, and try for equal weight. Shape, too, is important. A bulkier pannier masquerades as a heavier one, because its size moves the center of gravity outward. A slight imbalance, noticed on the trail, is easily corrected. Just put a small stone in the side that rides higher, or shift a little gear from one pannier to the other.

   Normally the panniers simply hang from the saddle. Before you load up—don't forget this—tighten both cinches. They'll loosen during the first mile up the trail, and they're hard to adjust when covered by the packs. Don't choke the horse, but tighten them a little more than snugly. Then adjust the straps to fit over the two wooden Xs. It helps to have a companion hold a little upward pressure on the first pannier while you're loading the second,

Mule packed with soft panniers on sawbuck.

so that the saddle won't pull too far toward the loaded side while you're getting its mate attached. Once both panniers are hanging on the horse, attach the belly strap underneath the horse, and snug it up. This setup may not be as professional or as foolproof as some of the hitches used by advanced packers, but it works well. Keep the packs balanced, and keep that belly strap snug—it too will tend to loosen.

With any horse or mule I've just packed, I take a few minutes to lead the horse around to see how the packs ride. A companion can eyeball them for you, seeing to it the two Xs on top of the saddle stay centered. That's more important than whether the packs ride at exactly at the same height. Also slap the packs with your hand and push them around a little. The horse needs to know they're there. You don't want him to be terribly surprised the first time he rubs one on a tree.

Hard panniers should be approached the same way, and as grizzly bear populations expand in the West, more and more areas require that food be stored in bear-proof panniers. Such panniers are tested by grizzly bears in a facility near my home. Particularly odoriferous food is placed in the test pannier, and if the grizzlies can't get into it, the panniers are certified. The alternative in food storage areas is to hang your food high and away from tree trunks, a tougher task than it may seem. Bear-proof panniers are a good idea in nongrizzly areas as well, because black bears and other critters tend to flock toward accessible food.

Just keep in mind that hard panniers are more likely to injure you or your horse in an accident. If a pack animal you're leading bolts forward, the pannier can strike your leg. If a packhorse or mule falls on such a pannier, a broken rib might result. I'd suggest putting hard panniers on your most reliable animal.

TOP PACKS

For greater capacity, panniers on the sawbuck saddle have long been supplemented by a top pack. Here's where the packer's art has traditionally come to play, because the top pack is often secured by one of several variations of the diamond hitch that look incomprehensible to the novice. If you're in that category, you're not alone. On a hunting trip to the Big Horn Mountains with his foreman in 1884, Theodore Roosevelt confessed that he and his employee were not experienced packers, not versed in the diamond hitch. Consequently, a good portion of their gear became scattered through timber and downfall, but with much repacking, no doubt by trial and error, TR and his friend eventually made it to camp.

The several versions of the diamond hitch all fit their namesake, because the ropes on top of the pack, actually on top of the tarp which covers the pack, form one or more diamond patterns when tied. These hitches are best learned in a hands-on packing workshop, though excellent written sources exist. I'm partial to Francis Davis's helpful *Horse Packing in Pictures*. The book is now between printings, but many used copies exist. Like most seemingly mysterious things, the complexities of the diamond hitch will tend to fade when you immerse yourself in learning it, preferably with a good helper.

But top packs that don't require hitching at all are available. Many now come in the form of a fairly flat, large, zippered pack outfitted with straps and buckles that secure across the top to the panniers. The fact that using these requires no knots whatsoever is convenient, but it has its downside. In a wreck, when a packhorse is pinned somewhere and struggling to rise, the traditional packer can rely on a sharp knife to get the animal out of a jam. If he's used three-strand rope for his sling ropes and he has traditional skills, he can take a quick break on the trail and splice the ropes, repack, and head up the trail. Cutting web straps, however, leaves no easy option for repair.

In any case, keep the top pack light. Put heavier items in the panniers and lighter ones in the top pack, so that you don't raise the load's center of gravity too much. Make that mistake and you'll someday have a very undesirable wreck. Should the cinches loosen, the packsaddle, panniers, and top pack might all swivel down under the animal's belly. I'll leave the rest to your imagination.

Jon checks on mule with soft panniers and buckle-on top pack.

THE DECKER AND MANTIES: MY PREFERRED SYSTEM

In the early days of mining in western Montana and central Idaho the need evolved for a saddle more rugged than the sawbuck and, more importantly, one capable of packing angular, odd-shaped, and very heavy mining equipment without injury to the packhorse or mule. The saddle that resulted had two bars similar to that of a sawbuck but with iron hoops commonly called D-rings rather than wooden slats connecting the two. Brothers by the name of Decker saw the first of these saddles in use, improved upon the idea, and even applied for a patent which apparently was never granted. However, the name stuck.

The saddle that bears the brothers' name is a remarkable piece of engineering. If you strip it to saddle tree alone, the primary difference is simply that iron hoops rather than wooden "sawbucks" fasten the two wooden bars together. But that change not only increases strength, it makes adjustment possible, though only by a skilled individual who can use a torch to heat the steel hoops and then bend them to change the angle of the bars. The sawbuck can only be adjusted by rasping wood off the bars to make them better fit an individual animal. (That method is also used with Decker saddles.)

Fitting over the saddle so that the iron hoops protrude (the visible portion is in the shape of a D-ring with the curved portion up) is a blanket-like device called a "half breed," which is built with pockets that allow padding to be installed. The traditional padding was horsehair, but some half breeds are now made with foam padding. On each side of the half breed is one of the Decker's most valuable assets, a hardwood board fitted into pockets that runs horizontally on each side of the pack animal. This board protects the animal from unyielding loads such as wooden pack boxes, by spreading out and distributing the pressure.

A pack pad is used under the saddle, just as with the sawbuck, but combined with the additional padding of the half breed and the weight distribution provided by the horizontal boards, the overall picture is one of an animal that is considerably better protected than he would be if carrying the same load on a sawbuck. And the advantages don't end there. The Decker is normally single rigged, but its single cinch is adjustable fore and aft. We normally like to adjust ours to the "center fire" position, the cinch hitting approximately the center of the rib cage.

The iron hoops on top of the Decker, along with the historic need to pack odd-shaped objects, have given rise to a whole different tradition of packing. Yes, you can use a Decker for panniers and top packs just as you can a sawbuck. To prevent the need for unbuckling the straps on the panniers to thread them through the D-rings, you can buy Decker hooks which you install on the straps so that they can simply be hooked onto the D-rings instead. Also, there are modified Decker trees whose hoops are square rather than round, with sides that angle inward. These are intended to work more like the wooden sawbucks, holding panniers when their straps are simply placed over them.

But as a way to pack up your assorted gear, the manty system has many advantages. You're not limited to items that fit into panniers, so it's no problem to pack in bales of weed-free hay or tentpoles and cots just a smidge too long for panniers. The system is quick and relatively easy to learn, and the gear needed is inexpensive.

The word "manty" is derived from the Spanish word *manta* meaning "blanket." "Manty" used here has several purposes. It refers to a tarp, usually

A Decker packsaddle on a mule, rigged for tying a basket hitch.

The versatile Decker can carry awkward loads. The wheelbarrow and the poles are for forest service projects volunteered by Backcountry Horsemen.

canvas, approximately seven-by-eight feet and also to the load you bundle up into it, and finally, as a verb, to manty up a load. Besides the manty tarps you'll need manty ropes, one for each load. I like 3/8-inch three-strand poly ropes around thirty-five feet long, with an eye splice tied in one end, a back splice in the other.

The mantied load is nothing more than a neat, normally rectangular package bound together by half hitches. Start by laying the load onto the manty tarp diagonally. The load itself can be many small items, but it works better to have them contained in boxes or bags. If there's a chance the manty ropes will dig into the load, say between a sleeping bag and a clothing bag, it works well to put stiffeners such as tentpoles or smooth sticks along the sides and top of the miscellaneous items.

For years I used open-topped plywood boxes for mantying. They made a neat load, and their open tops meant the load wasn't restricted to the depth of the box. Lately, though, to save weight I've used a simple sheet of half inch plywood, edges rounded off with a sander to protect the tarps. As a further improvement, I've installed a small shelf on the bottom of the plywood sheet, not really necessary, but handy.

With the load assembled on the tarp I fold the bottom corner up, then one side and the other, and finally the top down to act as a rain flap. Circling the manty lengthwise with the manty rope, I locate the eye splice on top of the manty, so that running the loose end of the rope through I create a big lasso, which lets me tighten the rope by lifting and bouncing the load several times. Then, I make a loop in the rope, invert the loop, and flip it over the top of the manty, which forms a half hitch around the load, which I pull tight. Then I do this a couple more times, finally bringing the rope around the back of the load, over the top, and tying it off.

The two mantied loads you sling onto the pack animal should be as close in weight and shape as possible. I used to believe I could detect weight differences within a couple of pounds by carefully lifting each manty, using the same posture, and raising the loads with the same flex of my arms; I can still come pretty close. But a packing scale works better. We weigh each manty several times and try to get them within five pounds or so, then, after slinging them onto the horse, insert a shovel or axe through the manty ropes on whichever side is lighter.

However, the Decker/manty system gives you an alternative. By slinging the heavier load just a bit higher you bring it closer to the center of gravity, and that can compensate for the weight difference. Shape, too, is a factor. A fat manty might weigh exactly the same as a thin one on the other side of the animal, but it will still tend to pull the saddle in its direction, because it's

Clinic clients mantying a hay bale.

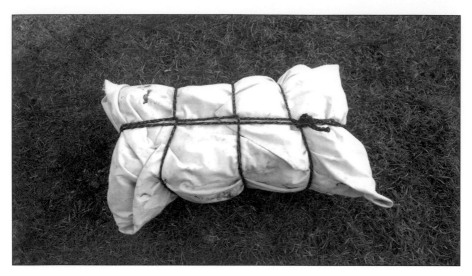

Completed manty ready to load.

farther out from the animal, and thus has greater leverage. Again, you'll probably want to sling the fatter one just a little higher.

Of the many ways to sling a load onto a pack animal, the basket hitch is probably the simplest and easiest to tie. I use it almost exclusively. But first, a clarification. The manty rope with which you've tied up your bundle has no role whatsoever in attaching the load to the animal. It exists exclusively to hold the manty, the neat package you've tied, together. The sling ropes on the Decker are larger diameter, a half inch instead of 3/8, and I like them to be a different color, as well. That avoids confusion when tying and untying the hitch.

Typically, one end of the sling rope is permanently eye-spliced to the D-ring, this mirrored on the other side of the saddle with the opposite sling rope. Perhaps because I'm left-handed, I usually set up my Decker saddles with the sling ropes eye-spliced to the D-ring on my right. To prepare to sling the load, I create a large loop in the rope, draping the rope down several feet, then inserting its end into the D-ring on my left, from outside in (left to right in this case). The end of the rope then drops toward the ground behind the loop.

I pick up the manty and lean it on the horse at approximately the right height, perhaps a third to a fourth of its length above the animal's back, and I bring the loop I've made up around the manty. I joke with clients that a bit of "packer's shelf" (potbelly) is handy for holding the manty in place as you tie the hitch. Reaching under the manty I grasp the loose end of the rope and pull hard, which tightens the loop around the load like a noose. Usually I like the loop to tighten around the manty about one third of the way down from the top.

I pull again, really hard. Then I bring the loose end of the rope up from the bottom of the manty and tie it off to the horizontal rope that's resulted from my pull. I usually use just two half hitches, doubled. Sometimes I'll tie a single slipped half hitch at first, then load the second manty. As while loading panniers, it's good to have a helper who can exert a bit of upward pressure on the first manty until you have the second in place. Then, with both in place, after I've walked the animal around to check for balance, I tie the second half hitch. Some packers use a quick-release hitch for this attachment, but I find the two doubled half hitches pretty quick to untie.

Also, packers in some areas tie a hitch that limits the swing of the manties, but I prefer to leave them with only the basket hitch attached and free to swing. I find that the "give" this provides is desirable when the pack

Hitching the load.

Pulling hard on the rope coming up from the bottom.

animal walks too close to a tree—the manty swings but returns to position after you go on by.

I earlier used the analogy of mushroom hunting when tiptoeing into the world of packing. Learn something, become good at it, and then move on if you wish. But if you find a mushroom you really like, and you have no huge desire to move on to other morsels, that's perfectly okay. From my interaction with packing friends and especially fellow hunters, I find that most learn a system that works for them, then just get more and more competent at it, learning additional skills only when and if a need arises.

The basket hitch can be used for other loads as well. The mare Chica is carrying two treated timbers per side, duct taped together, then basket hitched.

My "perfect mushroom" in this case is the Decker/manty system on most of my pack animals, using the basket hitch, supplemented with panniers attached to a sawbuck or Decker on another animal in my string. My bear-proof food panniers usually go onto a Decker. Although I enjoy learning other skills such as those involving packing bridge planks for the forest service as a volunteer member of Backcountry Horseman of America, the two simple systems described above take care of my own needs extremely well.

ON THE TRAIL WITH PACK ANIMALS

It's good to hone packing skills at home, but eventually it's time to get out beyond the round pen with these as well, and that involves skills for the rider

The author leads two packhorses packed with Decker saddles and manties into a bow-hunting camp. Note, arrows (visible on author's left) are very dangerous cargo.

and both the pack animal and the horse that leads him. No matter how much we do at home, we still have to get the critters out on the trail for real life experiences, and we have to see how well our packs stay put and whether our animals handle that occasional issue that is sure to crop up.

Ideally all our horses (and mules, for that matter) should be equally at home both packed and ridden. If, in spite of your best efforts, your favorite saddle horse develops a sore, it's nice to be able to leave him on the highline for a day while you ride another animal. Or perhaps the packsaddle will pressure him in a little different manner, its overall weight with loads somewhat less than your own weight combined with a riding saddle. Packing for a day rather than carrying a rider can be a rest for him.

We train all our colts to get used to packsaddles, but like most horse-men, we develop our favorite saddle horses, perhaps never packing them again. The biggest problem that arises is that your old favorite, even if he's totally comfortable with a pack, thinks he belongs with only you on his back, and he doesn't take to well to the idea of being ponied along.

Little Mack had become my go-to guy—cow horse, hunting horse, a gelding to whom I trusted my safety in several dicey situations while alone. But when he reached middle age I began riding a succession of younger animals, hoping to make each as safe and versatile as he was. On one mountain trip I elected to ride a huge gelding named Skywalker, young, a little green, but far enough into training to be trusted to lead a pack string. I'd pack Little Mack with panniers.

Little Mack was fine with the packsaddle and load, even though he hadn't worn one since his earliest days in training a decade earlier. Actually, he was probably delighted with a load far lighter than his big Norwegian owner. But he wasn't happy at all with being ponied along, a second-fiddle role as far as he was concerned. My right arm grew tired from jerking his lead rope and commanding "Back!" as he tried to progress alongside me on the trail. He was smart enough to veer back onto the trail on narrow or tree-lined portions where he had no choice. But as soon as the trail widened he was right there beside me again. Only the most severe whacks to the nose could have altered the situation, and I didn't want to be that hard on an old friend.

Too stubborn and also reluctant to reward him for bad behavior, I refused to stop on the trail, unpack him, and switch roles between Skywalker and Little Mack. But he ended up getting his wish on the return trip for an entirely different reason. We retreated from camp in a blizzard. Crossing an eleven-thousand-foot pass in a blizzard is serious stuff. I felt justified in relying on my older, well trained horse, so I elected Little Mack to lead the pack string safely over.

But the experience nevertheless points to the fact that you should work to train your horse to be equally comfortable ponying another animal or being ponied himself. When ponied, he should understand he's in a different role. Flicking the lead rope and commanding him to get back can be taught in the arena, then applied on the trail.

I currently have two delightful young geldings, full brothers—Chief, a gray, and Scout, a lit-up sorrel roan with socks. My goal is to have two geldings equally comfortable in both roles, ponied with packs and leading another animal. This may involve some challenge, since Chief is considerably more ambitious than Scout. But at least I can see to it that being ponied along isn't a role completely foreign to Chief.

Leading pack animals involves some potential wrecks, and most experienced packers will admit they've suffered a few of them, so let's start with some dos and don'ts. Obviously, it's best to get your feet wet by leading just one animal. Stringing pack animals together can wait until you (and they) have acquired some experience. If you're with companions, sometimes it's best that each rider lead a pack animal until all are comfortable on the trail; only then consider stringing them together.

Remember the number one worry I expressed early in this book, the caution against doing anything that somehow ties you to a horse that could entangle you? Stick with that. Don't ever tie a pack animal fast to your horse, the saddle horn, or anywhere else. When first ponying an animal, and always when you go through a treacherous section of trail, simply hold the pack animal's lead rope in your hand. Don't wrap it around your hand either, though it's okay to double the rope for a better grip. Although cotton lead ropes are a nuisance in wet, freezing weather, their large diameter makes them easy on the hand and pleasant to hold. I often use one on the animal in the front of the string.

When things become routine and comfortable I'll often pass the pack animal's lead rope over the horn, inside the pommel, then drape it down under my right knee. (For some reason it's always been more comfortable for me to neck rein my horse with my left hand and hold the lead rope in my right.) The rope in that position can be freed instantly, and I get an early warning signal should the packhorse pull back—the rope begins to slide under my knee and I can grab it.

When the terrain is very safe and my animals are gentle and trail wise, I'll sometimes take a single dally (wrap) around the saddle horn, knowing I can release it very quickly if need be. But, as your confidence builds, leave the dally for later. The only other time I dally is when a young horse or mule needs a nudge to follow me over a minor obstacle. Give him time on a slack rope, first. But occasionally the animal needs convincing that it's his job to follow, and that's where training accomplished earlier, involving pulling a load from the saddle horn, comes to play. That training has prepared your horse for the sensation of pulling from the horn. In such a situation take a single dally with your thumb in the air and apply pressure gently and intermittently, giving the pack animal the slack he needs to cross that puddle that's intimidating him.

But the biggest change you must make while leading pack animals, especially if you're an ambitious rider, is to slow down. The more animals in the string, the more potential for a whiplash effect, similar to what we experienced as kids during a "snake dance," once a popular parade-type activity at schools around homecoming. The front students didn't have to move very fast to create a major problem for those in the rear—the motion was multiplied.

Most saddle horses like to accelerate up the far bank after they cross a stream, and you must hold your horse back from doing so. Go over each obstacle gently and slowly, if necessary stopping briefly on the other side while the pack animals negotiate the obstacle behind you. Look back to make sure all step over that log in turn.

When stringing animals together we normally use a breakaway link between the pigtail on the packsaddle and the pack animal's lead rope. The purpose is simple—we don't want one pack animal to spook and pull the rest over an edge during an accident. It's better he break free. The pigtails on my packsaddles are 3/8 inch rope; the breakaway link is a quarter inch, natural fiber (sisal) not nylon or another synthetic, which would be too strong. Some people use baling twine for the purpose, but the plastic type is sometimes excessively strong, and since the stuff comes in various weights, strength is hard to estimate.

We don't want the breakaway link to be too weak, especially if we have a green animal in the string that is likely to balk briefly at a new challenge. Particularly if you're alone, getting off to reattach the animal frequently can be a nuisance, even a dangerous one in certain situations. Also, a spooked animal could leave the string and be lost, and short of that, allowing him to break loose too easily could train him to pull back. For this reason on the first training session I'll sometimes pony a very experienced pack animal and tie a green one directly to the pigtail, dispensing with the breakaway link. I'll do this only on easy terrain, most likely in my home pastures. But out on the trail I'll use the link made from a quarter inch sisal, which seems to be just the right strength.

Packing can be taught in the arena or corral, but it must be *learned* on the trail. You'll have the occasional mishap. A pack will come loose or an animal, even though well prepared at home, will act up in the new surroundings he's expected to assimilate. Real packers don't laugh at the mishaps of others, because they remember their own! Keep your cool, and don't try it alone, at least not at first. A companion riding behind the packhorses is incredibly valuable. He or she can watch the sawbucks or D-rings on top of the saddle and see to it they stay centered, the most important criterion. If something doesn't look right, stop and fix it sooner, rather than later. Problems with packs quickly multiply. Your companion says the pack on the rear mule is pulling slightly to the right. You figure you can fix it in a few minutes, when you find a better place to stop. Then suddenly, the pack is under the animal's belly, and you just hope his disposition is the best sort, that he'll hang tough and wait for you to fix the problem. With luck, by taking action right away, you can stop in a nice stand of timber where you can tie all your animals and work on the problem, a much better scenario than trying to fix things on the switchbacks of a steep ascent or descent. But take action quickly.

A final tip: packs tend to stay in place better when heavy and when the animals are headed upgrade. A majority of my own problems have come while going downgrade, especially with light packs. You're coming home

Note that the heavier manty has been slung higher to compensate.

Experience is only gained by doing it! On every trip you'll learn something.

from a camp, and having consumed your canned goods and other heavy items, the packs are light. Your animals know they're going home, and after inactivity on the highline, they're frisky. That's when things come loose. Don't get complacent simply because your loads are lighter.

Learn the art and science of packing piece by piece as needed, but don't be intimidated. Do it, just do it.

CHAPTER ELEVEN

FOR WANT OF A NAIL: A NOTE ON SHOEING

W e've all heard the rhyme. This is Ben Franklin's version in *Poor Richard's Almanac:*

For the want of a nail the shoe was lost,
For the want of a shoe the horse was lost,
For the want of a horse the rider was lost,
For the want of a rider the battle was lost,
For the want of a battle the kingdom was lost,
And all for the want of a horseshoe-nail.

But scholars tell us various versions of this tale go back much earlier, all the way to the thirteenth century, when iron shoes were just beginning to appear. Iron was expensive, though, and bronze had been previously used and probably continued as the material of choice until the manufacturing of iron became more commonplace. And long before that, recorded by the Greeks and others, early horsemen found ways to protect the feet of their heavily used animals, probably with early versions of the "Easy Boot," rawhide or heavy leather boots that fit over the hoof.

The verse as we know it reinforces the old-timers' statement, "No foot, no horse." It postures the idea that failure of a single horseshoe nail, should it have occurred on the horse of a military messenger, could result in loss of a battle and possibly even a kingdom. By Ben Franklin's time, horsemen in modern nations had come to believe that protection for hooves was the key ingredient in keeping their horses sound.

Now, however, we're being told that horseshoes have been a two-thousand-year mistake that with a regime of constant trimming, along with various toughening exercises and proper diet, a horse should never need shoes. "Barefoot farriers" (an oxymoron in the opinions of many traditional farriers) often prescribe what's called a "mustang trim," a foot trim that mimics the shape of feral horses running free. Sounds logical—or does it?

It's true that what we refer to as "free-roaming horses" are either feral or the offspring or descendants of feral horses. Although the term "wild" is often used to describe these equines, it's incorrect—all horses in North America are descendants of those domestic horses brought here by European immigrants, whether early from Spain or England and other countries later in the game. The only native North American horses were a tiny species, which along with an ancestor of the camel, served as a food source for Native Americans. Both of these species became extinct around ten thousand years ago.

That said, many bands of free-roaming horses have existed long enough for a certain amount of natural selection to take place. What has happened to the animals that had hoof problems? Unable to keep up with the herd, they've likely fallen victim to predators such as mountain lions or to the natural dangers of their environment, cliffs, rivers, starvation and other pitfalls too tough for a lame animal to handle. And, these unfortunate members of the herd haven't likely reproduced. So a band of free-roaming horses that's been established for some time probably is composed of tougher-than-average individuals.

But there's more to it than that. These horses are not asked to carry heavy riders. They aren't expected to walk or trot on pavement, nor are they asked to pull wagons or carts. They certainly never have to race against a clock or take a rider through a three-day-event course. They can avoid the worst footing if they wish, whereas the horse in use by humans has little choice. The free-roaming herd can adjust its speed, resting when it wishes.

Bone, too, is an issue. We're told by experts that in the quest for beauty, too often connected with a small head and petite feet, humans have bred much of the bone out of domestic horses in the last centuries. We're all familiar with the "big body, small feet" syndrome, the 1,200-pound horse that wears 00 size shoes and has tiny cannon bones. Such horses don't stay sound in domestic use and would probably succumb to predators quite readily if left to keep up with a free-roaming herd.

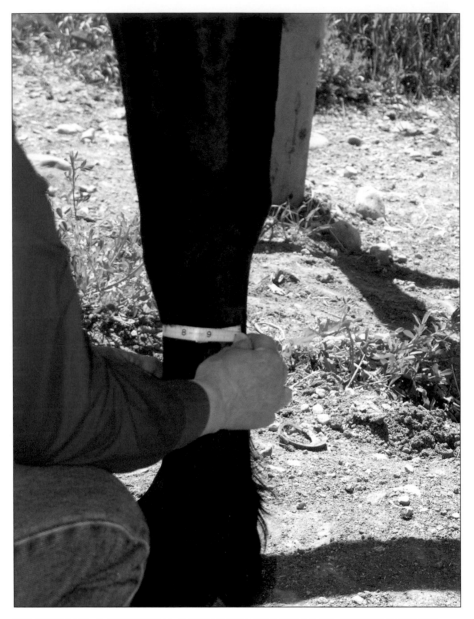

Measuring bone. A circumference of seven inches per 1,000 pounds of weight is absolute minimum—eight inches is better.

Certainly the ponies of the Plains tribes did well without shoes, but again, natural selection was part of the equation. Also, the Native American "cayuse" is virtually extinct, due to government-led mass slaughter of tribal horses shortly after the beginning of the reservation era. These horses were small and not particularly attractive, but did have magnificent bone. A few good photos of them exist, and they look very little like the idealized vision most have of the mustang or even of the feral horses of today.

For me, the comparison with free-roaming horses simply isn't valid. Yes, I'm sure that in certain uses on certain surfaces many horses can get by just fine without shoes. I certainly don't discount the research done in this area nor the sincerity of those involved in it. I'll own that I'm influenced by the fact that though the barefoot trend has been around now for quite some time, you'll still see police horses, performance horses, and particularly, backcountry horses, shod. The people whose lifework involves keeping their horses sound still gravitate, for the most part, to a horseshoe or something that offers an equivalent level of protection.

Although one case doesn't prove a principle, the experiences of one of my clients are of interest and they could have been tragic. A very sincere young man of modest stature and light weight bought a wonderful young mare from me. His ambition was to ride across the country from west to east. Although he wasn't an experienced horseman, he learned quickly, asked relevant questions, and seemed up to the task.

But if there's any field of endeavor whose followers fall easily to the pull of peers and the latest trends, it's the world of horses. The mare the young man bought had wonderful feet, and I sent her freshly shod by a master farrier to the man's temporary home in a nearby Montana city. There he would take lessons, condition the mare, and get ready for his trip. I told him the mare would need new shoes just before the trip, and that he was welcome to bring her down. Otherwise, I could recommend a good farrier near the stable where he housed the mare.

I soon learned the young man had listened to the siren song of a barefoot farrier who, perhaps for the publicity that could result from a cross-country trip made with one of his charges, convinced him that he could indeed cross the United States with a barefoot horse. I did everything I could to impress on the new horseman that he was contemplating a trip that was murder on feet. "You'll be riding on gravel, on pavement, and especially in barrow pits along the highway on a slanted surface where you'll likely encounter everything from broken bottles to chunks of wire."

My entreaties weren't convincing enough. After following to the letter the prescribed regime for toughening, including constant trimming, diet, exercise, and conditioning, the man had his horse trailered to the West Coast and began his journey. I didn't know the exact date of his departure, so I can't remember just how much time passed before I received a heart-breaking phone call.

He had reached the border of Nevada. He had led the mare for more than fifty miles and he had done so at a snail's pace. Her feet were so sore she could hardly walk. He told me it was with great effort that he could get her to walk without stopping for one hundred feet, so he would progress that far, then rest, then try again.

Totally tied up with commitments, I couldn't follow my first impulse, which was to hook up a trailer and head south to help him. But the young man must have been living right, because he staggered into the ranch head-quarters of some very nice people. They took him in, called their vet, and arranged for their farrier to evaluate the situation. The vet prescribed stall rest followed by pasture rest, and when the mare's feet had grown out suffi-ciently, shoeing by the farrier. In the weeks that followed the mare fully recovered, and the ending is happy. The young man did indeed cross the continent, later, to spare his own body, buying a light cart and harness and training the mare to pull it. I give him much credit for grit. But his near calamity could have been avoided.

Obviously, one case does not constitute an indictment of a whole philosophy of foot care. But it points to a larger issue, and one I see in train-ing trends as well. We should have some respect for our forebears. Most of them survived thanks to horses and mules, using them for both their trans-portation and their occupations. When you hear that something's been done all wrong for hundreds of years, think twice about such a sweeping state-ment. The old-timers often knew things "never dreamt of in the philosophy" of many horse owners today, because failure to know actually endangered their survival.

I'm old enough to fondly remember interaction with men and women born in the late nineteenth and early twentieth centuries, people whose life-work meant daily interaction with horses as their work companions. They always spoke of their experiences with a touch of nostalgia and with great affection for the animals on which they depended for their livelihood and survival. None had seen a training video, and only few had read a treatise on training. Yet, their knowledge was astounding, based as it was on accumulated equine wisdom passed down through generations and reinforced by their own experience.

The late George Miller, a draft horse guru I knew well, told me that one of his proudest accomplishments took place during a winter when he was a young man in need of work. A logger needed teams of horses, and he needed them before spring breakup, by the first of March at the latest. Around Christmastime, George was brought a herd of rank part-draft animals, none trained, four to six years old, right off winter range. He told me that by the deadline he had eight gentle teams (sixteen horses) trained and ready to go. He also said that at the time he didn't consider it any sort of big deal. How many horsemen do you know today who could accomplish that?

A similar respect for local knowledge is in order. Look at the feet of the horses and mules used by outfitters and forest service packers who do their life's work in backcountry and wilderness. Ask them how their animals are shod, by whom, and why they've developed their particular preferences. You'll see very few barefoot horses in these roles. Mules fare just a bit better, but they, too, are normally shod. The need isn't imaginary.

Your horse's basic training, as discussed earlier, should have included much handling of the feet: leading by them, tying them up, and so forth. Long before your young horse meets a farrier, you should get him ready by simulated shoeing, by tapping a small stone or another hard object against his foot while you hold it. Picking the foot up isn't enough—hold it up for some time, then, never drop it. Set it down gently.

When choosing shoes, or for that matter, Easyboots or another removable protective device, there's a trade-off between adequate traction and too much grip, particularly if your animal is not fully mature. During my high school and early college football years, we players wore extremely aggressive cleats on our shoes, removable metal-tipped plastic cone-shaped protrusions on the bottoms of the soles. On soft turf these sunk into the ground an inch or more and provided tremendous traction. They also provided terrible injuries, because when a blocker or tackler hit a player from the side there was no give. The foot was planted and couldn't move. The ankle or calf or knee did give, and the injury was often serious.

Football shoes today are quite different. Perusing the websites for high school sports outlets, I saw nothing like the ultra-aggressive cleats we were forced to wear. Modern football shoes feature very modest somewhat rounded cleats.

On the trails I frequent, which in many cases are ledges blasted from solid rock, good traction is extremely important. However, we still shoe our younger horses only with grooved "rims," not shoes with heel and toe caulks. We find that rims improve traction somewhat and definitely help protect the horse on trails that are rough and rocky in the extreme, but they do so without removing all the "give," thus protecting the pasterns of immature animals. Eventually I do use heel and toe caulks on mature horses, especially during fall hunting seasons when my horse must deal with snow, frozen ground, mud, and rocks.

Many of our trails are chiseled or blasted from solid granite.

For truly treacherous ground, especially in the case of ice, even more aggressive shoes can be used. Icelandic horses are actually exhibited on ice as slick as that on any skating rink, and for that special tungsten caulks are used. The old blacksmith shop on our ranch contains workhorse shoes with threaded holes into which the teamster could screw extremely aggressive caulks that protruded an inch or so below the shoe, driven into the ground or ice by the weight of the heavy horse. These were specialized shoes, used by people who had to feed their livestock with work teams on icy footing when the major fear was the animal falling and being unable to rise. Since workhorses normally only operated at walk or trot speed (only in western movies do the workhorses frequently gallop as they pull a conveyance) these ultra-traction devices did the job. But for speed events or normal use, they'd be hard on legs and terribly dangerous to the horse or human who happened to be kicked by one.

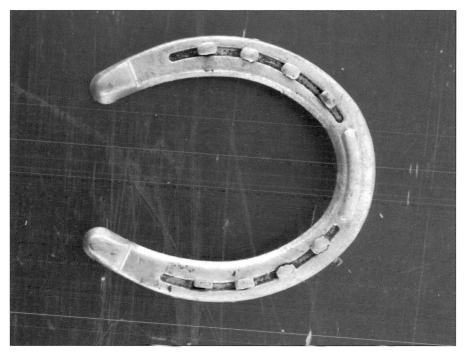

A horseshoe that's been pulled for winter. Note heel and toe caulks, not recommended for young stock, and holes to accommodate four nails per side. Except in unusual cases, all holes should be used.

Borium can be used for traction on horseshoes as well. Still another choice, one I've used when relying on a saddle horse for spring calving on icy surfaces, are tiny spots of hard-surface material welded onto shoes with existing caulks. The welding rod used is made of extremely hard steel. My farrier shapes the shoe first, because the welding process hardens the metal and makes altering the shape difficult. But again, these are shoeing approaches for extreme conditions, and I don't normally recommend them.

I'm not an expert on hoof angles. The farrier's task is complex, a delicate combination of both art and science. A well-shod hoof simply looks right. The shoe seems integral, the angle of the hoof natural, following that of the pastern. But I do see several tendencies that concern me, and if a farrier attempted them on one of my horses, I'd have some questions and prohibitions. Here are some cautions.

1. Some farriers trim the frog away, cleaning the hoof so that it looks hollow from the bottom. The hoof may look nice, but the farrier has removed one of nature's built-in shock absorbers. The horse needs that frog on the rocky trails you'll frequent.

2. Some farriers trim the heels down too low for my taste. That alters gait in subtle ways.

    But among gaited horses the greatest error I see, particularly in horses shod by farriers in the South who cater to the show community, is leaving too much toe on the hoof. I don't mean the extravagant, exaggerated hoof treatment used by "big lick" folks—a terrible blight on the reputation of the Tennessee Walking horse (that is no fault of the horse). I'm referring to what some southern farriers consider "light shod," still with too much toe to be a safe proposition for our Montana mountains.

    A Tennessee family stayed at our ranch some years ago. They brought some nice horses, and I'd made it clear to them that for our trails, the animals needed to be light shod. But I took one look at their animals and shook my head. Each was wearing a shoe that protruded at least an inch farther forward than it should have. I suggested they make an appointment with my own farrier, but they objected, since they'd just paid to have all their animals shod.

    On the first ride up the trail toward one of my favorite lakes, one of their horses fell flat, twice. This was partly due to his inexperience in rough country, but more was due to shoes made to catch every rock and twig. He was the equivalent of a hiker wearing size 13 shoes when his feet were only size 9. The family reluctantly reshod their horses to a backcountry standard, and they had no further trouble.

3. The opposite error, shoeing that leaves part of the shoe trailing behind the hoof, is equally problematic. This results when a farrier uses a shoe too large for the hoof, narrows it on his anvil, and tacks it on. The portion protruding behind the hoof is a natural hook to be snagged by a rock on the trail, either loosening the shoe or pulling it completely off.

4. The nail holes in shoes are meant to be used. The shoes my farrier favors have four nail holes per side, and I want to see a nail in each. An exception must be made for that rare hoof that's so vertical on the sides that it's hard to make the fourth (rear) nail work without "quicking" the animal. But if your farrier consistently tells you the shoe will hold just fine with fewer than the available holes, tell him no, it won't, not where you're going.

5. Some farriers routinely use a sedative on a horse the instant it acts up slightly, perhaps attempting to take a foot away; this is something virtually all horses do occasionally. First, I want no one medicating my horse without my express permission. The farrier who routinely sedates horses is saving work and effort, but only at the horse's expense. I doubt whether horses learn much while under sedation. That said, the owner can't have it both ways. If you allow your horse to abuse the farrier he has every right to walk off the job. I'd rather see a farrier get a little tough with my horse once, teaching him something, than have to go through an unpleasant experience each time the farrier attempts to drive a nail. And, when that nail is driven, there's a moment of serious danger before the farrier has a chance to twist off the protruding point. Farriers without a good number of scars on their hands and wrists are rare.

    On those occasions when a sedative is actually needed, Dormosedan Gel has worked well for us. We've used it more than once after a colt's encounter with a porcupine. The gel is not to be swallowed—instead it's placed under the tongue and allowed to dissolve. Rubber gloves are in order.

6. For a shoe to stay on in backcountry conditions, where your life could depend on your horse staying sound, the nails have to be

clinched, hard. I like to see a farrier's forearm muscles strain when he clinches nails, after initially setting them with hammer and block.

7. Lastly, the general principle in horseshoeing, whether by the hot method (when a shoe is forged) or cold with "keg" (standard production shoes) is that the shoe is shaped to the foot, not the opposite. The farrier trims the hoof to be fitted with a shoe. Then he makes a shoe or modifies a premade shoe to fit the foot. This principle is increasingly violated by the new "pre-fitted" shoes and farriers who install them "as is." Every horse's foot is uniquely his own. I want to see the farrier fit my horse, not adjust my horse to fit what's in his pickup's cargo box. I expect to see a farrier unload an anvil when he shows up, evidence that he plans to shape shoes.

I'm not dismissing alternatives to the iron shoe for horses. Yes, boots can work. Under some conditions the barefoot routine, if followed to the letter, might work as well, especially in areas with relatively friendly surfaces and deep topsoil. But keep in mind that the backcountry horse operates in a different world than the competition animal or the backyard horse kept and ridden in an urban area. At an arena competition, farriers (and for that matter, veterinarians) are likely to be available. But backcountry riding requires self-sufficiency, and being "in want of a nail" can have serious consequences. Help is not available at the touch of phone button, and there's no veterinarian on call.

I do take an Easyboot along on backcountry trips, choosing a size that will fit my largest horse. How would I hold a boot this size on a smaller hoof? Laugh if you will, but the answer is "duct tape," the modern equivalent to the rancher's baling wire as a solution for a host of problems.

But best, of course, is prevention. Find a first-rate farrier, one whose shoes *stay on*! Treat your farrier well, and don't let your horse abuse him. Prepare your horse for the farrier by constant attention to his feet. Pick them up and clean out any stones or dirt before riding. Constant handling of your horse's feet trains him for the farrier and lowers his stress when it's time for shoes. And yes, do give your horse some barefoot time, perhaps in winter or during any other stretch of time when you won't be riding in difficult terrain.

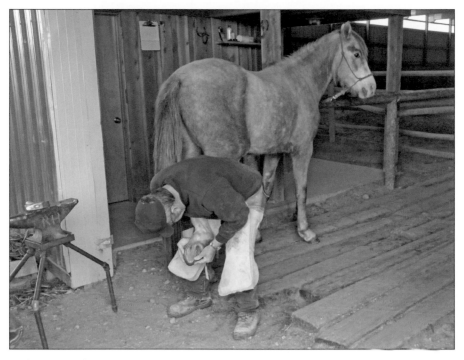

Find a good farrier and treat him well!

CHAPTER TWELVE

THE HIGHWAY TRAIL: TIPS FOR TRAILER TRAINING

Unless you're lucky enough to live adjacent to the backcountry in which you ride, backcountry trips will normally begin with a trailer ride for your horse to the trailhead. Of course, horse ownership in general requires trailering to the veterinarian, for a change of pasture, or to a competitive event. I'm old enough to remember a day here in Montana when more horses were transported in cattle trucks than in trailers. Every trailhead had a ramp for unloading your horse, and should you need to unload him where no ramp existed, you found a steep bank such as a railroad grade, backed the truck as close as you could to the upward slope, and jumped your horse out of the truck, the slope lessening the distance from the truck bed to the ground.

I never remember an issue with loading a horse into the back of a cattle truck when a cattle ramp, heavily built with corral poles on each side, was used. The ramp smelled of livestock, and the truck bed itself was spacious, much like a corral compartment.

Some horses were trained to load without ramps at all. We bought our first walking horse mare nearly forty years ago. She was a big mare, taller than sixteen hands and nearly ready to foal. At the time I owned only a pickup truck with a stock rack mounted on the bed, a fairly common setup in those days.

When I arrived at the ranch to load the horse after a deal had been completed by telephone, I looked around in vain for a loading ramp. The outfitter from whom I was buying the horse said, almost scornfully, "You don't need no loading ramp." He led Mona to the back of the pickup, and I pulled the rope to raise the gate. The outfitter said, "Load, Mona!" The mare half-reared onto her hindquarters and jumped into the back of the pickup;

the vehicle bounced on its springs under the weight of the big mare, then settled down. Previously worried that I'd paid too much for the mare, I decided then and there that I'd paid too little!

Unlike the rather spacious and open beds of cattle trucks, trailers are too much like caves, and no horse is initially enthusiastic about walking into a cave. Horses are open-country animals. They don't like confinement. They're always looking for an escape route, so walking into a tight space without a clearly visible exit goes against their grain.

Trailering problems can be created as well. If a horse bumps his head on his way into a trailer he's not likely to forget it. A rough ride the first time a horse is transported will tend to make him leery of another.

Of course, not all trailers are the same. What are called stock/combination trailers usually have partial walls with open area above them, sometimes set up to close with Plexiglas for cold weather. At the other extreme are two-horse side-by-side trailers and even one-horse models, not seen too often today. These are the most confining and most likely to make your horse pause.

There are two general approaches to training horses to load, one which uses considerable pressure, another which relies on taking one's time and familiarizing the horse with the trailer to lessen his fear. You've probably seen the former demonstrated at clinics, often with horses that are reluctant to load. A skilled trainer uses a long lead rope or a whip to make the area outside of the trailer uncomfortable for the horse. I emphasize "skilled" here, because someone clumsy in use of the rope or whip can do more harm than good.

The trainer creates a circle of discomfort around the horse by use of the whip or rope, only occasionally touching the horse with it, whirling it, cracking it, but only spanking when necessary. He then reduces the size of the area of discomfort until the horse jumps into the trailer as a preferred alternative to being harassed outside of it. Then, if the trainer is doing this correctly, he or she allows the horse to come back out of the trailer, then load again, repeating this several times, each time with less hassle. The method has the advantage of teaching the horse to load without being led into the trailer, a safety plus.

This system works, and it can be very effective. Alas, with some horses it's not particularly pleasant or low-stress. The horse decides the trailer is the

With skillful use of the long lead rope, trainer Mike Lorash trains a young filly to walk into a two-horse trailer. Afterward, he let her back out and load again repeatedly until she was completely comfortable with the trailer.

Such training pays off—Emily sends her gelding Scooter into the trailer.

lesser of two evils. With enough repetition he'll tend to settle down, decide the trailer isn't as terrible as he thought, and all will be well.

But early trailer training usually eliminates the need for a high-pressure approach. Loading weanlings after they've been halter trained, perhaps using a rump rope (a good tool for halterbreaking generally) can prevent stress later. We often load foals along with their mothers for a change of pasture. Usually they jump into the trailer behind their mothers, and the mystery of the trailer is gone.

Mostly we use step-up trailers, rather than ramps. With a ramped trailer, make sure the ground you're on is as level as possible, and test the ramp with your own weight before loading a reluctant horse. If the ground below it isn't square and the ramp tends to wobble, put a rock or a block under the corner that's not touching the ground. The more solid the ramp, the less likely your horse will have problems with it.

In an impasse situation, when the horse stands at the rear of the trailer and simply stares, afraid or unwilling to take the first step, we'll sometimes lift a front foot and place it up onto the trailer, encouraging the horse to do likewise with his other front foot. Do this carefully, working from the side. Sometimes it's enough to convince the horse he can go where you've placed his foot.

Make sure the horse has a clear path into the trailer, and make the interior as bright as possible. Don't block the horse's avenue with your own body. A woman once purchased three yearling geldings from me, all of which had been loaded a few times into a trailer. Her particular trailer was one of those with a rear tack room (which I don't care for) that blocked off half of the rear width of the trailer. She grabbed the lead rope of the first colt, walked up the ramp, stood in the doorway of the trailer, turned toward the colt while tugging on the rope, and let loose with a litany of, "Come on baby, it's okay. Really it is. Be a good horse . . ." etc., etc.

Finally, when I could get a word in edgewise, I said, "He might load if you get out of the way." In a bit of a snit, the woman handed me the lead rope and stepped off the ramp to the side. The colt walked into the trailer, and his buddies followed him.

I'm not afraid to apply a little pressure when needed, particularly with an older horse that "knows better." A friend purchased a horse named Blaze from us and had used him for several years, so I was surprised by the call one morning when he planned to help me move cattle. Frustrated, he told me in colorful language that he couldn't get his gelding to load. He lived only four miles down the highway, so I told him I'd be right down.

What I saw as I pulled in was the classic impasse, my friend standing holding a lead rope, obviously trying to coax the gelding into the trailer, the horse standing impassively, not moving. But I also saw the horse watching me carefully. Believe me, horses know vehicles, and he recognized the pickup. He also recognized me. I got out swinging a rope coiled in my hand and walked toward Blaze and the trailer, then had to suppress a laugh when the horse took a last look at me and jumped into the trailer.

Of course, my friend thought I was some sort of a magician, or perhaps a fearful personage to the horse, but I was neither. Blaze was bluffing. Perhaps he was just a little out of sorts that morning and not particularly anxious to go to work. His owner told me the horse had brushed his ears on the ceiling of the trailer the last time he'd loaded, not bumped his head but merely touched the trailer ceiling enough to make him duck. Perhaps that was the excuse. When I arrived he knew the jig was up and he'd just as well load.

It's always safest to send a horse into a trailer, rather than lead him into it. The training routine that drives a horse forward against an arena wall or corral fence pays dividends here. Either with the end of a long lead rope or with a longe whip, you gradually decrease your horse's circle until he's asked to pass between you (or another object) and the arena wall. With this as a preamble, you can send him into the trailer using the same technique. Especially with smaller trailers, the most dangerous place you can be is in front of a horse in a tiny trailer. Should the horse suddenly pull back hard, right after you've tied him, his front feet will go into the air. When the lead rope snubs up he'll come forward, right on top of you.

If instead you can send him into the same small trailer, secure the butt rope, and then tie the horse via the feed door in front, you've saved yourself a potential wreck. Unfortunately, many of today's larger trailers pretty much require you to be in with the horse in order to tie him or to secure his slant stall. Even with these, it's best to send the horse in first if you can, and that's a training goal worth pursuing. And all trailers, of any size, should have an escape door up front.

Similarly, it's much the best if the horse learns to back out of the trailer, even if it's a large one. Backing, both from the ground with the lead rope and from the saddle should be well instilled into the horse you're riding. In the trailer, be stubborn and take your time. Back the horse and give him some time to feel out the rear edge of the trailer or the ramp, if one exists. The horse's caution about stepping off an edge to his rear is understandable—the edge is in his rear blind spot, and his instincts tell him the drop-off could be a cliff. But after a few times, horses catch on. Give him some time to feel for the ground with that first hind foot—then all will be well. A couple of my older geldings practically run backward when unloaded. The issue with these horses is making them *whoa* in no uncertain terms while I untie them, and for safety's sake staying in front of them.

If you allow your horse to turn around and walk out of the trailer, you must be in one of two places—either you get completely in front of him and allow him to turn, then walk out on his own, presumably to have his lead rope snatched up by your buddy if it's not long enough for you to retain, or you stay well back of the horse toward the rear of the trailer while he turns around. The position in between is dangerous. I once watched one of those slow-motion accidents that make you feel helpless—I knew it was about to happen but couldn't prevent it. My friend carelessly untied his mare in a stock trailer. She quickly turned, and with her own chest, pinned his against the trailer wall for just a second or two. He stayed back from the ride that day, nursing a couple of broken ribs.

The potential power in a thousand pounds of muscle, released in tight quarters, is something it's best to never experience. Writer Tom McGuane in his book *Some Horses* talks about being trapped in that situation, in front of a powerful Quarter Horse in a tight trailer, the horse blowing its cork. He was fearful for his life. By teaching the horse to walk into the trailer ahead of you and by cautious unloading, you can work to avoid such a situation.

Remember, too, that in a small two-horse side-by-side trailer, when loading hook the butt chain first, then tie. When unloading reverse—untie first, then release the butt chain. Releasing the chain first can send an unwanted signal to the horse that he's free to back up. If he's tied, a severe pullback and possibly a broken lead rope or chain, even a horse coming out hard and going over backward, is possible.

The interior of a trailer is an unnatural environment for a horse. Do everything you can to make it comfortable and desirable. (I reward my horses with a grain or hay treat after loading.) Work gradually to make your trailer comfortable and fear-free, and that extends to your driving as well. Slow down and accelerate as gradually as possible, take curves more cautiously, always remembering your friends are back in that trailer—keep it nice for them!

CHAPTER THIRTEEN

THE BACKCOUNTRY CAMP: LEAVE ONLY TRACKS, KEEP ONLY MEMORIES

I've traveled many miles of trails through backcountry and wilderness with my horses and mules, sometimes alone, sometimes with loved ones and friends. Always there has been a feeling I can describe only as intense and satisfying. Usually there have been butterflies in my stomach at the trailhead, accompanied by anticipation. Will the packs stay in place? Will the animals behave? Will there be trees down over the trail from that strong wind that blew last night? Better have my saw handy, either on my saddle horse or the front pack mule.

But that sensation goes away quickly as the animals fall into line, the packs ride well, and I begin to take in deep breaths of mountain air. There is satisfaction derived from the knowledge that my animals have been brought this far, have been trained to the degree that they can transport a well-equipped backcountry camp, my companions, and me over mountain passes, through roadless areas. Yet, I realize, that the training isn't done. It's never done. As long as I'm out here with my animals, they are learning and I am learning.

Yes, in a sense that saying about the journey also being the destination applies. To get well-trained backcountry horses and mules, you must take them beyond the round pen to the backcountry. No amount of training in a round pen waving a flag, no endless repetitions of exercises to build softness on the bit, no progression through various training levels can make a back-country horse. The old-timer's saying that it takes wet saddle blankets to truly train a horse comes to mind, and I'd add that it takes doing what you want the animal to be able to do.

Boxers have always approached their training a bit differently than many athletes in other sports. With some notable exceptions, few lift weights extensively or spend a great deal of time in what might be called "cross-training." Boxers tend to prepare themselves primarily by boxing. Yes, they jump rope, run, and shadowbox with punching bags. But primarily they box. Similarly, the ultimate training for the backcountry horse is hard work in the backcountry.

While we head toward camp we will likely experience new things, and we'll get through them. Maybe we'll see elk (to horses not too much scarier than deer) or a moose (often much scarier). We'll step over downed trees, encouraging our critters to step rather than jump over, for it's hard to tell whether there's safe landing on the other side. We may come suddenly upon a backcountry camp nearly straddling the trail, its big white tent flapping in the wind, woodsmoke emanating from a campfire or the tent's stove pipe. The low-stress-obstacle approach comes to play. We'll give our animals time to stare and assimilate, maybe moving sideways a bit if possible to get a better view, and when their breath returns to normal we'll go on by.

And while we train our horses on the way to camp, we train ourselves as well. We hope that any wrecks are minor ones, and from them we learn. The basket hitch on one side of a mule loosens and the manty on that side creeps lower. It's better to fix it sooner than later, and it's not that hard—loosen the knot on the hitches, pull a little slack in the horizontal part of the hitch, push the pack up, and pull the slack back out, renewing the knot.

While on the trail we can spread goodwill. When you meet hikers sing out, "Hello!" Doing so at first sight of them helps your horse as well. Perhaps the contour of the hiker and his or her backpack is incomprehensible to the horse, and the hiker's answer assures your animal that this strange moving object is indeed human. Smile (it doesn't cost anything) and show interest in whether the hiker is catching fish or having a good day. If you're engaged in some trail clearing or improvement, make sure to say so. But keep moving—don't visit while your animals grow restive. If you're on a hillside, gently ask the hiker to get off the trail on the downhill side. And don't take anything for granted. I once had a fisherman lay a fly rod across the trail in front of me as he cheerfully got out of the way, assuming my horse would gently step over it. I just as cheerfully suggested he move it to be useful on another day.

The day when a high percentage of our population had rural roots is long gone. Many hikers simply don't understand livestock of any sort. That's the other reason to keep moving. You don't want someone to approach your horse to pet it or even to grasp its bridle while you talk. Yes, I've seen that happen.

All travels have destinations, and the wilderness camp, our portable home, is waiting for us in just the right spot. We must find it, use it, and when we leave it,

A wilderness camp.

leave back as little trace of our stay there as possible. With horses and mules, big, heavy creatures that leave tracks and droppings behind, "leave no trace" becomes a challenge. But it's a challenge we must meet, for the forces that wish to lock us out of the wilderness are pervasive, rich, and powerful. One way to combat them is to join such organizations as Backcountry Horseman of America and participate in their many projects to assist the forest service and other agencies in maintaining and building trails. Government agencies are slaves to the whims of Congress and are too often underfunded. When hikers see horsemen packing in bridge planks or water bars or culverts, they tend to be more willing to overlook those horse droppings on the trail.

Recruiting youngsters into the ranks of horse lovers, helping them get away from their electronic devices, and building love for both nature and equines will pay dividends down the road. Yes, taking kids along involves more trouble and risk. But failing to do so will allow backcountry horsemen to become a dying breed, with the inevitable loss of political clout.

The most important thing we can do is maintain a good image and come as close as possible to the "leave only tracks" ideal. Let's start by choosing a location for that perfect camp. What we all envision is a location by a stream or a lake in a meadow with bountiful feed for our stock. Yes, water is important, but we must not locate either our tent or our livestock too close to it. Regulations vary, but a common requirement is for livestock to be kept two hundred feet from a stream or lake edge. Watering should be done a couple of times a day, all animals at one time, preferably in a location that provides easy and safe access to water but one that is rocky and less likely to be mucked up by hoof traffic. Avoid pristine-looking areas or those next to what appear to be good fishing holes. Leave those for backpackers.

For some reason horsemen seem to crave photos of themselves mounted on a horse or mule standing belly-deep in the crystal water of a mountain lake. Yes, this can make for a pretty picture, but what is the first thing a nonhorseman thinks of when he sees such a photo (or sees the picture-taking session in person)? He thinks of horse droppings falling into water on which he hopes to cast a fly. True, any pollution is probably a drop in the bucket and no worse than that left by a moose or an elk. But image and perception are everything when it comes to keeping our stock welcome in the backcountry. It's best to limit our water crossings to existing fords on the trail.

As to feed, finding that perfect meadow in which to graze may not be a realistic goal. In some wilderness jurisdictions, such as the east half of the Absaroka/Beartooth Wilderness Area, grazing is completely prohibited, in my opinion an overreaction years ago to an earlier use, that of sheep grazing in the high country, prohibited when the area was designated as wilderness. The result is that even hobbling or picketing to graze is unlawful, leaving just one option, packing in all feed and keeping stock tied to a highline continually. Packing feed means adding another animal or two to a pack string, causing additional impact, which is one of the reasons I think this regulation is shortsighted.

If you do need to pack feed, it must be certified weed-free. Stock users are often told to switch to such feed several days before entering forest service land, the theory being that weed seeds in the manure may sprout. (I'm told that recent studies question that theory.) In any case packing feed is often necessary during fall hunting season, when the snow is deep. We use pelleted feed that is certified weed-free and normally feed it in nose bags to minimize spillage. Certified hay cubes also work well. With either of these make sure your horse gets plenty of water. Both products are concentrated with much of the moisture removed and dehydration, especially of a horse that has worked hard all day, can become a cause of colic.

We also know those who pack certified weed-free baled hay into remote camps. Bales that weigh around sixty pounds each manty neatly and travel well. Until the horses consume them the bales make nice benches from which to enjoy the campfire.

Thankfully, most forest service and wilderness areas do allow grazing, and portable electric fencing probably causes the least impact. It's important that your horses are already trained to respect electric fencing—you don't want their first experience with it to occur miles from the trailhead when a spook and escape could have serious consequences.

Compact fencing units run on flashlight batteries or a small solar collector. Highly visible white tape, with tiny metal wires running through it to conduct electricity, combine with lightweight plastic fence posts to create an easily moved corral enclosure where horses can graze with the least possible impact to the ground. Before the grass is grazed to a nub, move the corral to a different area. We've also found that bungee cords double as insulators and fence tighteners. They can be rigged to trees without causing damage and stretched out to hook the fence material. But don't trust the electric fence to hold your horses at night. A deer, elk, or moose, can inadvertently run into the tape at night, panic, and knock the whole thing down. If that happens you'll be looking for your horses in the morning.

Hobbling is the next best bet in terms of keeping impact minimal. Picketing (from the front foot, as we've trained) is relatively light on the land, but only if you move the picket stake frequently. Otherwise your animal will graze an unsightly circle. The option today of leaving mules loose to be tended by a bell mare is available only in extremely remote areas where your animals are unlikely to annoy others. But it's a good system for high country wranglers in areas where it's feasible. The mules stick with the bell mare, and the wrangler need only fetch the mare in the morning—the mules will follow her in.

Tie to trees only very briefly—if at all—while you're unsaddling and dropping packs. A nervous horse or mule can paw out a cupped area around a tree in a remarkably short time. Hobbling while tied can help, but some animals can paw effectively, anyway. The cupped area can expose tree roots and do considerable damage to them. Abrasion of the lead rope tied around the tree is equally undesirable—it's very tough on bark. And horses like to eat the bark of certain trees, especially the young cottonwoods frequently found in creek bottoms out west. A horse can girdle a small tree in short order, killing it.

The highline has become the restraint method of choice, but it, too, can have impact. If possible rig it on higher, rocky ground. Use tree-savers (commercially available straps for the purpose) or extra cinches from the packsaddles to encircle the tree at each end. (If you use cinches make sure they're well brushed to remove all bits of bark before putting them back on a saddle.) Tie the highline high and tight, and tie your horses short enough to it that they can't reach the ground. The lead rope must contain a swivel, even if you use swiveled "knot-savers." You can avoid using any hardware whatsoever by learning to tie the picket-line loop, shown in the next chapter. If you camp in one location for several days, you should move the highline periodically, and in any case, repair the disturbed ground under it as well as possible. Break up manure clumps and shovel back displaced soil.

A highline in the wilderness.

Tree-saver.

Training to tie reliably, when accomplished at home, should make highline use relatively trouble-free, except for handling the horse that decides the highline provides a good opportunity to bully his neighbors. It's hard to get the highline loops far enough apart to completely prevent this if your string is large—you can only make the highline so long. I normally tie the loops (or install the fittings) approximately six feet apart, then tie the animals with around three feet of lead rope. That way one horse can't wrap around another.

Handle the bully situation by trying different arrangements of animals on the highline, and listen for squeals that indicate conflict. Dominant animals should be placed on the ends, with their tying loops farther away from others. In spite of the criticism often dished out to mares, we've actually had more problems with older, crotchety geldings in this regard.

Campfires can also be a source of unsightly scars. The ultralight method we used as backpackers involved removing a section of sod and putting it aside, digging a small hole, burning only paper and wood (no foil or cans please), and enjoying a small fire. To reclaim we'd drown the fire,

This highline utilized metal fittings rather than highline loops. A fitting can be seen between the two horses.

scatter the ashes, replace the soil and the sod, water it to help the grass resume growing, and through these efforts make nearly all traces of a fire disappear.

Even that method has problems, though. The fire does change the pH of the ground, and in heavily used campsites the whole area can become pockmarked with reclaimed fire pits. In such areas, though it's always been discouraged, someone has probably made a fire ring of rocks, which have become blackened and unsightly. But if such a ring exists, use it. There's no sense in creating more disturbance—better that all fires are built in one place.

Some other options include building a campfire on fireproof blankets, often available for free from the forest service or some fire departments. These blankets are designed as last-resort protection for firefighters should a wildfire change direction and overrun them. In such a horrible scenario, the firefighter pulls the silver blanket over him and hopes for the best. To offer such protection, fire blankets must be in perfect condition. Those used for drills sometimes develop small cracks or holes and must be withdrawn from inventory. Our local Backcountry Horsemen unit was given a batch of these to use under campfires. Yes, some grass will still be killed by the heat transferred through the blanket, but the fire is safe from spreading and its impact on the ground is minor.

All backcountry areas these days operate on the "pack it in—pack it out" principle. The bad days of garbage pits behind frequently used camps are, thankfully, gone forever. When a campfire is permitted you can burn paper products. But cans must be smashed, and along with foil wrappers and all sorts of other garbage, put in heavy duty plastic bags for transport out. In food storage areas that require either bear-proof panniers or hanging food high above the ground, garbage must be protected the same as food. Animals that become habituated to human food and garbage are not only dangerous, they're on a path of self-destruction. Conflict with humans will eventually result in their demise.

In wilderness country human waste is still most frequently dealt with via the "cathole" method: sod removed, a hole dug one shovel-blade deep, waste then buried with only toilet paper and the sod replaced. Group camps of longer duration call for a latrine approach, and your local forest service jurisdiction should have recommendations for construction of these. In all cases the site selected should be high and dry, well away from any streams. Should you have a dog along, treat his waste the same as human.

Doing everything we can to minimize our impact and that of our animals keeps the backcountry a place we truly want to go. But in addition to its aesthetic benefits, being light on the land helps stem the tide of opinion against the existence of horses and mules in the backcountry. Try to avoid travel at inopportune times, for instance on muddy trails after spring rains, when tracks become holes and a heavily trod area can be left looking like a feedlot corral. Be courteous to hikers and other users—they're after a fulfilling experience as well, and they vote! And volunteer if you can. Opinions about equines in the backcountry often change readily when people see pack animals carrying planks to replace a bridge or volunteers with two-man crosscut saws clearing the trail for everyone's benefit.

CHAPTER 14

SOME ESSENTIAL KNOTS

Often considered the bible of knots, the *Ashley Book of Knots* contains nearly four thousand of them. That's an astounding number of knots, but thankfully, your life as a backcountry horseman can become better and safer by learning only a tiny fraction of them.

In the days when sailing ships handled the bulk of cargo needed by humans, sailors were the ultimate experts in the world of knots, and for this reason many knots bear nautical names. A sailing ship contained many miles of rope (line, to a sailor), so much rope that hemp, grown for the fiber needed to make it, was a major farm crop during the sailing-ship era.

But when it came to knot expertise, cowboys and packers were no slouches. Their work, as well, required familiarity with dozens of knots and hitches. Yours as a recreational backcountry horseman requires relatively few, but those few are very important. For a more complete treatment I refer you to my book *The Pocket Guide to Equine Knots* and to the several fine books mentioned at the end of this one.

A good knot has two simple requirements, and the second is too often forgotten. First, it must hold. Your life could depend on that. Second, it must be relatively easily untied. Otherwise, the rope is ruined and probably must be cut. Here are several of the knots I've found most essential as a horseman and packer.

SQUARE VERSUS GRANNY

The square knot is probably the first knot a Boy Scout learns. It can also be tied with a slipped loop on top, or with two slipped loops. The square knot tied with two slipped loops is the knot with which you tie your shoes. Or maybe not—if they frequently come untied you're probably tying a granny knot with two slipped loops.

A square knot looks like two loops hitched together. It can take a bit of pressure and still be untied relatively easily. It's a decent knot with which to tie two ropes together, but only if the two ropes are the same diameter and texture. I use square knots constantly, a typical use being to tie a safety rope around a post and gate when I fear a clever mule might figure out the latch.

Square knot.

Grasp the two ends and pass one end over and under the other. Bring the ends up toward you, and going the opposite direction, again pass the same strand over and under the other. Do the second step wrong and you get a granny knot. It's worthless—it won't hold, and if it does, it'll be very hard to untie once it's been pressured.

Granny knot.

To tie a slipped square knot, pull a loop of rope over and under the other strand instead of inserting an end. You now have a knot that's relatively quick to release. In all cases pull both sides of the knot tightly in opposition to each other to make the knot secure.

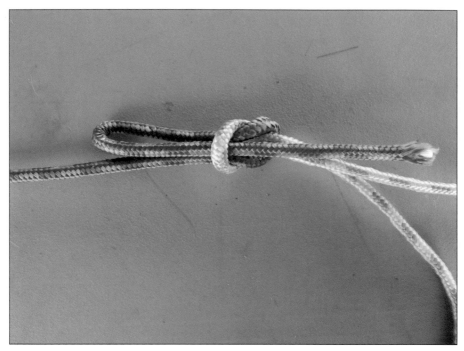

Slipped square knot.

THE SHEET BEND

Lately, I've been using this knot a great deal. Named for its nautical use (sheets are the lines on a sailboat that adjust the sails), the sheet bend is at its best when a steady pressure on it is maintained. It's better than the square knot for joining two ropes together, especially if one rope is larger than the other. If you tie a rope halter correctly, you're completing a sheet bend already started for you by the halter manufacturer.

Make a loop in the end of one of the ropes, the larger if the two are of unequal diameter. Bring the end of the other rope up through the loop, go around the doubled rope, then out under itself. Pull tight. Go in the direction that allows the ends of both ropes to be on the same side of the knot.

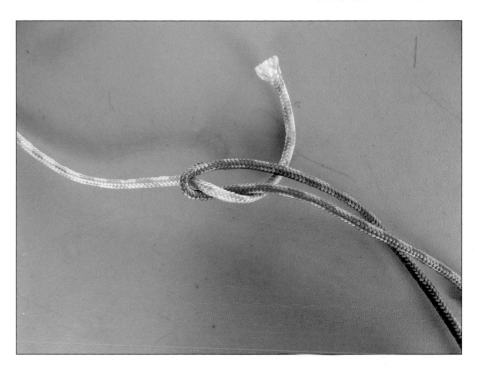

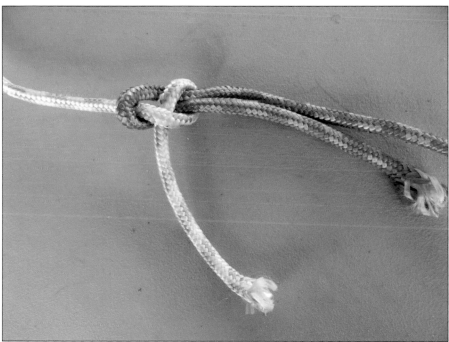

Sheet bend.

Properly tied halter completes sheet bend.

In tying a halter, come up through the standing loop from below, and complete it the same way. Really, you're tying a half hitch around a loop which jams into the loop—that's the secret of a sheet bend's strength. Yet, it's easy to untie.

THE BOWLINE

This is the queen of all knots, so revered that an entire book has been written about it. The bowline's special and most valuable characteristic is that it creates a fixed loop that refuses to slip. A bowline can be tied around the axle of a truck and no matter the pressure exerted while the truck is being pulled out of the ditch, the bowline won't slip, and it can actually be untied afterward.

This feature makes it invaluable for the horseman. I use it around the base of a horse's neck when I tie up a rear hoof. Or, I tie it toward the top of his neck in an emergency and lead the horse home. In a crisis situation, a horse caught in a bog, for instance, the bowline is the knot to use when you fasten a rope around his torso. Tied around your own waist the knot is equally reliable, and pressure won't cut you in half. You can use a bowline for a tie-up knot if you wish, and two bowlines, one looped through the other, make a strong connection between two ropes. If there's any knot that should be taught by all horse clinicians, it's the bowline.

Start by laying out a loop of any appropriate size. Then, twist the rope to make a small loop and bring the end of the rope up through the hole made by the small loop (the rabbit comes up out of the hole) and circle the standing part (the rabbit goes around the tree), then stick the end back down through the hole made by the small loop. Pull it tight. Practice this knot until tying it becomes second nature, because in an emergency, it's likely to be the knot you need.

Start bowline with a loop.

Rabbit goes down the hole.

Rabbit goes around the tree and back out the hole.

Completed bowline.

TIE-UP KNOT

Many knots work for tying your horse securely, and you can use a bowline. However, a slipknot is better in some respects, because when you loop it around a post (or briefly, a tree) it will tighten and help prevent the knot from slipping lower. Here's a handy one I use.

Wrap the lead rope around the post or rail and bring the end back toward you. Twist to make a small loop with the standing portion on top. Then simply place that loop under and on the other side of the span of rope between the horse and the post. Create another loop (called a bight) and pass it through the smaller loop you made. Pull it all tight, noticing that the knot will slip up against the post. You can make several more bights, each time passing them through for added security if you wish. Finally, place the end of the lead rope loosely through the last loop you've made.

Tie-up knot, step one.

Tie-up knot, step two.

Completed tie-up knot with quick release. Pass end of rope loosely through loop as a hedge against the Houdini horse or mule, then remove that and pull for quick release.

To untie, take that end out of the loop and simply pull one time for each increment of the knot you made. This is a quick-release knot, though keep in mind that most quick-release knots can still be difficult to untie if a great deal of pressure (i.e., a horse pulling back) has been put on them.

TWO HALF HITCHES

A half hitch is a foundation for many other knots. You begin a square knot with a half hitch and probably tie one without thinking by putting the working end of your rope over and under the standing part. If you double the end before inserting it over and under, you have a slipped half hitch, handy for a quick temporary tie.

Slipped half hitch, good for quick, temporary tie.

Tying two opposite half hitches next to each other results in the lanyard hitch and also the latigo hitch, the traditional knot used to tie up the cinch latigo on a saddle before cinches were buckled. I use two half hitches in this manner as a handy way to secure the reins of my horse to the saddle horn. I bring both reins up on the near side of the horse, lay the reins around the saddle horn, and pass them under the standing portion, then make a twist to form another loop, which I pass over the horn.

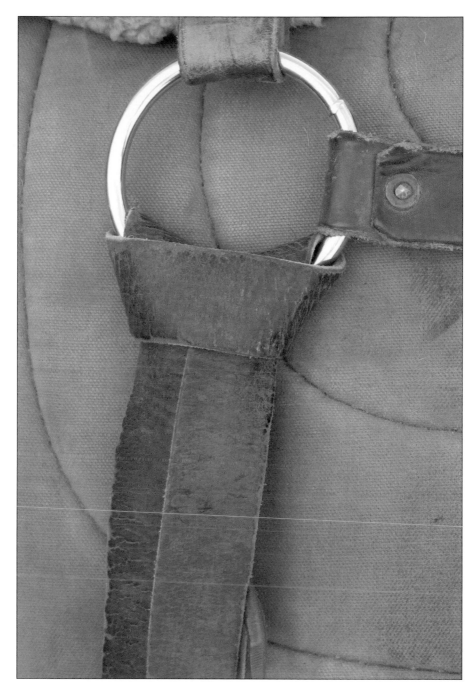

Latigo (also lanyard) hitch consists of two facing half hitches.

Two half hitches around horn, step one.

Two half hitches, step two.

Two half hitches, step three.

A series of single half hitches secure a manty, as discussed earlier, and they can be used as well to drag a set of poles or firewood logs back to camp. Start with a lariat loop around the bundle, then tie a series of half hitches around it leading in the direction of the pull. The half hitches will all tighten together.

A slip loop plus several half hitches allows dragging a bundle of boards or poles.

CLOVE HITCH

This knot is similar to two facing half hitches except that the two go in opposite directions. To make a clove hitch make a small loop in your rope by twisting, then make a second identical one. Then place the two together, one on top of the other. Place the double loop you've made over an object and pull the two ends in opposite directions to tighten.

Clove hitch, step one.

Clove hitch, step two.

Clove hitch around saddle horn, complete.

The clove hitch is handy when you want to tie the center of a rope onto something and provide resistance in each direction. You can tie the middle of a rope to the saddle horn of your riding saddle and rig a basket hitch, especially if your saddle has holes in the cantle as mine does.

PICKET-LINE LOOP

Although you can buy metal fittings for your highline that nullify the need for loops made by tying, you can save weight with this simple loop knot. Yes, you could make a loop in the rope and tie a simple overhand knot, but once such a knot took pressure you could never get it untied.

Tie by making a loop in the line with one clockwise turn. Then place the loop up under the standing portion of the line to your right so that the top of the loop you've made projects just above the standing portion. Now bring the bottom of the loop up through that slot and pull everything tight. The loop you start with should be fairly large, because as you pull things tight its size will be reduced.

Picket-line loop, step one.

Picket-line loop, step two.

Completed picket-line loop.

The picket-line loop works just as well as the metal fitting when used to make a "Dutchman." Tie one in your highline about six feet from the tree on one end, pass the end of the highline rope through the ring on the tree-saver, and then back through the picket-line loop. Now you have a two-to-one mechanical advantage for pulling the highline tight.

Dutchman, here using a metal picket-line loop fitting.

EYE SPLICE

Eye splices are easy to tie and have a multitude of uses. I use them to make the loop holding a swivel for a lead rope, or, to make a lead rope with no swivel—I can just pass the loop through the ring on a halter and pass the end of the lead rope through the loop, then pull tight. My manty ropes have an eye splice tied in one end, as do my sling ropes. You can create an impromptu lasso with a rope that has an eye splice tied in one end.

Eye splices are easy to make with any three-strand rope. (I use three-strand ropes exclusively, just for this reason.) Start by unraveling six or eight inches of the rope at the end. If the rope is quite stiff and or of the sort containing strands that easily separate, it can help to wrap the ends of the three main strands with a bit of tape.

Make the eye of the splice as large as you like. Then insert the middle strand under and back out of one of the strands in the standing part of the rope. From there on it's easy. Rotate the rope and continue to progress by tucking your unraveled strands over and under successive strands of the standing part. If you do it right, it will look right. If you accidentally tuck two strands of the unraveled portion under the same strand of the standing part, just back off and fix it. Four tucks per strand are adequate for natural-fiber ropes, but with slicker synthetics it's best to go five or six. Roll the rope under your boot when you're done to make it look better.

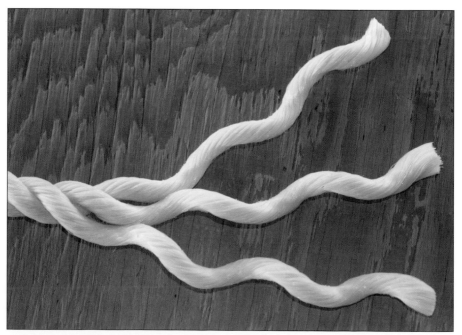

Steps in tying an eye splice.

CONCLUSION: KEEP LEARNING, KEEP TRAINING, BUT GO!

The author.

I write this in the midst of Montana winter. The snow is deep, and the aspen groves are months away from first leaf. South of me the Beartooth Mountains blaze with white, the alpine winds whipping up clouds of blown snow around the peaks, the snow sifting into the pines, banking moisture that will recharge our creeks and rivers throughout next summer. There will be no packing over the passes until well after the Fourth of July, and the snow will be deep on the trails over some of them for weeks after that.

Our horses and mules paw range grass saved for their winter feed, except for the youngsters and the training crew, fed close in to be available for those days mild enough to allow some meaningful work. The two young molly mules that packed in camp last fall are slated for a new challenge, work in harness, eventually to pull a wagon and sled. Never through this winter will a single day pass when I won't touch a horse or mule, feed many of them, and enjoy hearing them munch their hay. And always I'll be thinking of warmer days to come when the trailheads beckon to me and to horses whose winter coats have given way to spring sheen.

The purpose of this book has been less to teach than it has been to prompt the reader to learn. Many of its chapters could be books in themselves, the subject of each nearly limitless in scope. But my hope has been to give you a nudge, along with enough information to set you free from the mental and physical confines of the round pen and the arena. The round pen and the arena are wonderful schoolrooms, and much can be learned in them. But I was always the school boy who kept his eye on the plate-glass windows, at the view of the hills that fringed our valley. And that's where I headed whenever I could, just as soon as the school bell rang.

Train your horse well, but get him out there. Head toward valleys where no highways run, toward creeks that have no bridges. Camp in the pines and listen to your horses enjoy their feed on the highline. Get out, as my farrier said, where they'll really learn something. And when you can't, when the snow is deep and the temperature below zero, reading about it is a healthy substitute.

Here are some useful books: As an author I'd be foolish not to recommend several of my own. Three of them, *The Complete Trail Horse, The Pocket Guide to Equine Knots,* and *101 Trail Riding Tips,* will prove useful companions to this book. For packing information I've always liked *Horse Packing in Pictures* by Francis Davis. I've been known to photocopy some of its pages and pack them along to camp in case my memory needs jogging when a particular knot or hitch is needed. *Horses, Hitches, and Rocky Trails* by Joe Back is an old-school delight, entertaining in both its verbal descriptions and its illustrations. (Don't expect political correctness.)

Especially strong in the Decker/manty approach to packing, *Packin' in on Mules and Horses* was written by Smoke Elser and Bill Brown, pioneers in the organization of Backcountry Horsemen of America. And there's much to be learned from reprints of several military instruction manuals including *Horse Packing: A Manual of Pack Transportation* by Charles Johnson Post.

The renewed interest in mules has sparked many good books. There is a fine anthology (to which I contributed a chapter on gaited mules) *The Natural Superiority of Mules: A Celebration of One of the Most Intelligent, Sure-Footed, and Misunderstood Animals in the World,* Third Edition, by John Hauer. In it you'll find dozens of stories about mules, particularly as used in the West and in the backcountry, along with many beautiful color photographs.

Keep your horses happy and your hitches tight—see you in the backcountry.

INDEX

A

Absaroka/Beartooth Wilderness Area, 194
accessories mounted on saddle, 39–41
A-fork saddle, 43
amble, 101
American Gaited Mule Association, 143
Anderson, Clint, 125
approaching, side, 7–9
The Art of Horsemanship (Xenophon), 80
Ashley Book of Knots, 200

B

Back, Joe, 222
Backcountry Horsemen of America, 147–148, 165, 193, 199, 222
"Backcountry Navigator," 98
backpacks, 118
bad spooks, 58–59, 64
"barefoot farriers," 173
barn-soured horse, 62–63
basic backcountry riding, 63–67
basic trail training
    basic backcountry riding, 63–67
    good spooks, bad spooks and
        fake spooks, 56–63
    handling obstacles, 48–56
    open country and critters, 67–72
    speed control, 72–77
    tacking up and mounting, 42–48
basket hitch, 43, 150, 158, 162–165, 192, 215
Beartooth Mountains, 1, 221
beers, 72
Bennett, Dr. Deb, 98, 113
bicycles, 36
big lick gait, 102–103
Big Open challenges, 67–70
Billings, Josh, 139
bits, 80–82
bits/bosals, 45–46
bitting rig, 83
blind spots and spooking, 6
BLM (Bureau of Land Management), 69–70
Bob Marshall Wilderness, 105
bombproof, 56
bone (shoeing), 173–175
boots, for horses, 172, 182, 187
boots, importance of, 14–15
borium, 179
bowline knot, importance of, 23–24
breakaway systems, 32
breast collar, 132

breast strap, 152
breeching, 37
breeching/britchin, 148, 150, 152
bridling, 45–46
broad loin, 110–115
Brown, Bill, 222
Bubba the Gaited Jack, 143–145
bucking rolls, 43
bull snaps, 33

C
campfires, 197–199
camps, backcountry, 191–199
canter (lope), 97
Canterbury Tales (Chaucer), 101
cathole method (for waste), 199
caulks, 178–179
"cayuse," 174
center of gravity, 113–118
certified weed-free feed, 194–195
chargey (speed control), 74–77
Chaucer, 101
cinches and cinching, 43–45
clove hitch, 214–215
collection, 105
The Complete Trail Horse, 222
conditioning, 112–113, 118
Cowboy Mounted Shooting, 122
cow trails, 67
cows, 70–71
crossbuck. *See* sawbucks and
    panniers
crupper, 148
cruppers, 37–39, 150
curb bit, 81, 90–92
curb strap, 81

D
"dally," 131–132, 168
Davis, Francis, 155
Decker and manties, 157–165, 222
deer, 71
desensitization vs. sacking out,
    34–41
diagonal trot, 101
diamond hitch, 146, 155-156
direct rein, 79–92
Dormosedan Gel, 181
downhill riding, 65–66, 115
dragging loads from saddle horn,
    131, 213
dragging mishaps, 16
dragging mishaps, avoiding, 13–14
D-ring on saddle, 127, 150, 157-158,
    162, 170
"Dutchman," 217

E
Easy Gaited Horses (Ziegler), 100
Easyboots, 177, 182
"E-collar"/electronic collar, 124–125
electric fencing, 196
Elser, Smoke, 222
English horse, neck reining, 87–89
Equine Studies Institute,
    Livingston, CA, 113
"Essa on the Muel," 139
eye splice, 218–220

F
fake spooks, 60–62
farrier, 1, 3, 24, 31, 173–183
feet

leading by each foot, 20–22
picketing, 29–31
tying up a hind foot, 22–25
feral horses, 69, 173, 175
field trials, 120
"finishing" the rein, 89
fire blankets, 198
first ride, 84
flat walk, 99–100, 105–108
"flooding therapy," 129
foundation training
desensitization vs. sacking out,
34–41
feet, ropes and ties, 20–34
training gaps, 18–19
Fox Trotters, 106–107
foxtrot, 101
Franklin, Benjamin, 172
"free-roaming horses," 173
full cheek snaffle, 81–82

G
gaited, 100, 140–145
gaited breeds, 100–103
"gait-keeper gene," 102–103, 108
game (such as deer), accustoming
horse to, 129–132
Gehlhausen, Logan, 148
good spooks, 57–58, 72
good spooks, bad spooks and fake
spooks, 56–63
GPS, 99
granny knot, 200–201
graze rope, 16
grazing bit, 90
ground driving, 82–83

ground tying, 123–126
gunfire (hunting horses), 121–123

H
half breed (Decker saddle), 157
half hitches, 13, 24, 33, 160, 163,
204, 209-213
haltering, 10–12
handling game, 129–134
handling gear, 126–129
handling obstacles, 48–56
Hauer, John, 223
highline, 32–33, 196–198
hobbles, 25–29
horse breaker, 35
*Horse Packing: A Manual of Pack
Transportation* (Post), 223
Horse Packing in Pictures (Davis),
155–156, 222
Horses, Hitches, and Rocky Trails
(Back), 222
horses, nature of, 4–5
hounds, following, 120–121
human waste/cathole method, 199
hunting horse
ground tying, 123–126
gunfire, 121–123
handling gear and game,
126–134
overview, 119–121
Hunting Trips of a Ranchman
(Roosevelt), 104
hybrid vigor, 137

I
Iceland, 42, 47, 100, 102, 112, 178

impulsion/collection at walk, 72–75
Irving, Washington, 103

J
jennet, 100
on the job training, obstacles,
    52–56
"Josh Billings" (Henry Wheeler
    Shaw), 139

K
knots
    basket hitch, 162–165
    bowline, 204–207
    clove hitch, 214–215
    eye splice, 218–220
    overview, 200
    picket-line loop, 215–217
    sheet bend, 202–204
    square vs. granny, 200–202
    tie-up knot, 207–209
    two half hitches, 209–213

L
laggard (speed control), 74
lanyard hitch, 210
latigo hitch, 210
leading, 12–13
"leave no trace," 193
leg cues, 39, 41, 43
leverage bits, 80–81
light rein, 64
loops, avoidance, 15
loose rein/light rein, 64
low-stress approach, 48–51

M
Manitou, 104, 123
manty/manties, 158–165, 213
McGuane, Tom, 190
mecate, 15–16
Miller, George, 177
Mongolia, 100, 112-113
monocular versus binocular
    vision, 48
Montana Backcountry Horsemen, 102
Moore, Bill, 143–144
moose, 71
mounting, 46–48
mules, 135–145
"mustang trim," 173

N
nagging, 74–75
*The Natural Superiority of Mules:
    A Celebration of One of the Most
    Intelligent, Sure-Footed, and
    Misunderstood Animals in the
    World* (Hauer), 223
neck rein, 78–79, 85–88
"No foot, no horse," 172
non-leverage bits, 80–81

O
obstacles, on the trail, 48
101 Trail Riding Tips, 222
one-rein stop, 59–60, 72
open country and critters, 67–72
over-stride, 99, 104

P
pace, 101

pacey horses, working, 106, 108
packer boots, 14
"pack it in - pack it out," 199
Packin' in on Mules and Horses
    (Elser and Brown), 222
packing
    Decker and manties, 157–165
    overview, 146–148
    saddle panniers, 148–151
    sawbucks and panniers, 152–155
    top packs, 155–156
    on the trail, pack animals,
        165–171
packing feed, 194–195
panic snaps, 33
panniers, bear-proof, 155, 199
paso gaits, 101
Percheron, 116
Peruvian Paso, 108
picketing, 29–31
picket-line loop, 215–217
pigtail, 146, 169
plantation saddles, 42
"plow reigning," 78
The Pocket Guide to Equine Knots,
    200, 222
ponying, 18, 167–168
Poor Richard's Almanac (Franklin),
    172
Post, Charles Johnson, 223
Psalm 32, 80
pulling a load, 130–134
"pulling collar," 132

Q
Quarter Horse, 108

quick-release knot, 24, 33, 163, 209

R
Reagan, Ronald, 5
refusing an obstacle, 52
reins, 84–86
remuda, 35
rifles, 126–128
Roman cross-chains, 103
Roosevelt, Theodore, 35, 103–105,
    120, 123, 129, 155
rough country riding, 64–67
rump, passing, 6–7
rump rope, 31, 187
running walk, 74, 99, 101, 134

S
sacking out vs. desensitization,
    34–41, 123
saddle gait, 101
saddle panniers, 148–151
saddlebags, 115–116
saddles
    plantation saddles, 42
    western, 42–43
    western vs. English, 37
saddle scabbard, 39–41, 129
sawbuck pack saddle, 83
sawbucks and panniers, 152–155
scabbards, 126–129
sedatives, shoeing, 181
shanks, 81
sheep, 71
sheet bend knot, 202–204
shoeing, 172–183
side pass, 92–96

single-foot gait, 103–104
skills, 3
slick or A-forked saddles, 42–43
slipped square knot, 202
snaffles, 81–82, 90
Some Horses (McGuane), 190
soring (of Walking Horses), 106,
    120
speed control, 72–77
split reins vs. loop rein, 84
spooks, 56–63
SPOT, 4
spurs, 86–87
square gaits, 101
square vs. granny knots, 200–202
stepping pace, 101
survival horsemanship
    blind spots and spooking, 6
    boots, importance of, 14–15
    dragging mishaps, avoiding,
        13–14, 16
    haltering, 10–12
    leading, 12–13
    loop avoidance, 15–16
    nature of horses, 4–5
    rump, passing, 6–7
    side approach, 7–9
    trust, 9–10
swell or bulges, 43

T
tacking up and mounting, 42–48
tapaderos "taps" stirrup covers,
    13–14
Tennessee Walking Horse, 102,
    105–107, 134

tie-up knot, 207–209
tölt, 101, 112
Tom Thumb bit, 81
top packs, 155–156
trail, with pack animals, 165–171
trailer training, 184–190
training gaps, 18–20
trees, tying to, 195
trot, 97–99
trust, 9–10
"20 percent rule," 110
two half hitches, 209–213
tying, 31–34

U
uphill riding, 65–66, 115

W
walk, 97–108
Washington, George, 137
water crossings, 55
weekend clinics, 18–20, 34
weight variables, 109–118
"Western Pleasure" gait, 97
western saddles, 42
Wilderness Act, 36
The Wilderness Hunter, 104
working cattle, 89–90

X
Xenophon, 80, 105, 120

Z
Ziegler, Lee, 100